GETTING YOUR
MONEY
$HIT
TOGETHER

stop worrying about money
and live your best life

MAX PHELPS

RETHINK PRESS

First published in Great Britain in 2019 by Rethink Press
(www.rethinkpress.com)

Contents

Introduction

We all want more happiness in our lives and less worry. When we worry too much about money, it can be shit. When we are confident in our ability to pay bills, plan for holidays, have fun and know we will be able to afford the same level of comfort for the rest of our lives, then we've really got our money $hit together. This book is about being able to enjoy life, travel and do the things that are important to us now, while having a plan for a future that will allow us to retire comfortably by the time we hit fifty.

I love my life and my work and could have retired at forty-six. Instead I enjoy showing young people on a career path, how to get to the same point. Hopefully, by learning from my successes and failures, more people can get there sooner than I did.

I spent fifteen years building a career in a multinational and discovered that the more we earned, the more we spent. I have to say 'we spent' because my lovely wife of twenty-seven years, Kelly, is a much more talented spender than me. As I later learned, most people are more like Kelly in the way they like to spend than me, a card-carrying tight-arse (TA).

Our habits changed when, fifteen years ago, we set ourselves a goal to control our expenses and cover them with passive income so that we could retire. For me, retirement was about getting off the corporate ladder and teaching – that's really what I love and what I want to dedicate the rest of my life to. After eleven years of spending almost all of our income, I accidentally stumbled across a way to start saving and was ready to invest, but then four years later I got made redundant. I had to reconsider where I was going and what I was doing. Instead of getting back on the corporate ladder and sticking to my original plan, I decided to jump to my end game and get trained and qualified as a teacher.

I took a massive pay cut from working as an ex-pat director in a multinational to train as a teacher in the UK, but I loved it. After two years we came back home to Australia, but the UK qualification didn't enable me to teach here. Instead I decided to try mortgage broking until I could afford to take a year off to re-train as a teacher.

The more I listened to people's situations and looked at their finances as a broker, the more I realised how many people, like Kelly, just needed some better structures in place to be much better with money. Most people need to be guided in how to plan for the long term while enjoying the now. I now feel that coaching adults about money is a much more valuable mission than teaching Pythagoras to teenagers. The five-2 money diet is based on the discovery that we all need a minimum of five bank accounts across two banks to manage money. It has been thoroughly tested and proven successful for Kelly, so why not for you and your partner too?

By the age of 46, in 2014, we hit the point where our passive income exceeded our expenses, so we could have retired if we wanted to. Kelly took the opportunity to spend more time with our grandson, Matthew, who was born that year. But I decided to dedicate myself to coaching adults on the practicalities of how to manage their money and plan for a prosperous future. And that's what this book is all about. It's about sharing my knowledge and spreading the word to far more people than I can meet individually. Kelly taught me, a maths nerd and TA, to enjoy and appreciate the finer things in life. And she learned how to work to a budget, freed from the worry of bills and long-term planning.

My vision is to give people the confidence to make good decisions and to enjoy every year for the rest of their lives. That's when you know you've got your money $hit together.

The rest of this book is going to go through my five-P process for long-term financial freedom through investing in property. It's ok to dip in and out of the sections and chapters in the book, provided you read about the *Preparation* stage, which covers our revolutionary five-2 approach to money management that will change your life forever. The *Planning* and *Purchase* stages are important for anyone wanting to buy property. If you are a die-hard share lover, the *Portfolio* section will not be for you because it's about building a property portfolio. *Pay Down* might be worth skim-reading at first and revisiting later when you get to that stage in your life.

Along the way we'll also be talking about giving back, because studies show that helping others makes us happier (Dunn & Norton). I'm very proud to say that we have taken the 1% pledge on behalf of our companies, Golden Eggs Investment Services Pty Ltd and Golden Eggs Mortgage Brokers Pty Ltd. Pledge 1% (https://pledge1percent.org) is a global movement to get companies all over the world to commit 1% of their time, income or assets in support of the United Nations global goals. We actively support education in countries where it is more difficult to access than in Australia. By buying this book, a contribution has been made on your behalf towards educating kids in Zimbabwe, so thank you for this contribution; and as you read through, look out for other ways you can help us to contribute more.

ONE

Why We're Here

What we believe

I believe that everyone in full-time employment can get their money shit together and fund their own retirement. Not rely on government handouts. Not rely on their family members to support them. My calculations show it's perfectly possible to support ourselves and we only need to look at the fact that the minimum full-time wage after tax of $35k is more than double the $15k/year paid to cover the living costs of the unemployed and pensioners.[1] The only trick to it, though, is living our working lives on 80%

---

[1]   www.humanservices.gov.au/individuals/services/centrelink/
      newstart-allowance/how-much-you-can-get; www.fairwork.gov.au/
      how-we-will-help/templates-and-guides/fact-sheets/
      minimum-workplace-entitlements/minimum-wages

of what we earn – not what typically happens, which is living on between 95% and 105% of what we earn. Of course, the more we earn, the more we can afford to spend during our working lives and the more we can save to provide for a better retirement.

My second belief is that it's possible for anyone to learn how to organise their finances so they can both enjoy life now and prepare for retirement.

My third belief is that everyone needs an education and we need to keep educating ourselves. A lot of us leave school at 16, 18, 21, and then education stops. The problem is that no one teaches us about finances and budgeting and how to do a tax return. It's also difficult to find someone we trust to talk to about money. This book's not about doing tax returns, but it is about managing our own money and I think it's probably much more valuable than some of the other things that we learned in high school, like Pythagoras. When I was trying to teach 13-year-olds maths and they'd ask, 'How is this going to help us?' I had to sort of bumble through, saying 'It's the process of learning and the application of logic', or, 'Stay in at break time and we can discuss it further.' We really need to be teaching kids and adults, people of any age, how to be good with their own money.

And, lastly, I believe in great holidays. If and when we get to age seventy or older, and we look back on our lives, the things that we're going to remember after family and friends are the great holidays and experiences we had – the places we went, the people we met on the way. We're not going to remember the stuff that we used up and threw away in our twenties, thirties and forties. Unfortunately, when we look at where people spend their money, way too much of it is spent on takeaways, expensive clothes and gadgets. At seventy, all that stuff is just landfill. We might remember the odd one or two items of clothing or gadgets we had or the upgrades in the gadgets that we bought, but we're much more likely to remember our family, our friends, the things that we achieved personally in our lives, and the memorable stuff that punctuates our years, like holidays. When we go through this process of looking at how to live on 80% of our income, part of the 80% should be spent on travel or holidays.

My background

I wasn't born into money or wealth. I'm the third-eldest of nine children, with two older sisters, making me Big Brother. I don't consider nine ridiculously large, but yes, it is too many to fit in a family sedan, and no, we're not Catholic, plus we always had a TV (to answer the standard questions my family always gets asked).

One of the favourite games for the bigger kids to play on the many rainy days in England was Monopoly. My two older sisters and my mum's best friend's daughter, who was my age, and I would play for hours. I loved our games of Monopoly and had a gift for being very quick with numbers. I also had such a good memory that I didn't need to look at the card to know how much rent was due. I was often the banker. The game flows better when someone can take their own turn quickly enough to do the extra job of the banker without slowing things down.

Our mum, Josephine, an only child who grew up next door to a family of four kids around her age, made the career decision to have a family of six kids – a goal which she went on to overachieve. She would have liked more but started relatively late at twenty-seven. She used to say she was a 'household manager', a very apt description for a brilliant budgeter who made sure everything was paid on time and all of us were fed, clothed, had a home and even had an annual holiday every year without fail. She finally returned to work when the youngest turned five and started school, after an impressive twenty-two years on maternity leave!

My dad, on the other hand, always loved work – going from being a herdsman on a farm, to a milkman, then a self-employed bread rounds-man (which is like a milkman, but delivering bread, cakes and pastries door-to-door). By the time he'd moved on to being a delivery driver for a pie company, many of us had left home. When he married my mum, he told her he was no good with money and handed over his pay packet, unopened, every week. Back then everyone got a weekly envelope full of cash, with the 'pay slip' typically written on the outside of the envelope, often by hand.

During his self-employed years, my dad managed to earn below minimum wages, making my mum's budgeting skills seem even more impressive. But to be fair, realising at twenty-one that he was no good with money and delegating the role to his wife was one of the best financial decisions he ever made. He would ask her for pocket money to go to the pub, or to play cricket, which always ended in the pub too, and know that he was free to spend the money without worrying about bills, food, council rates, car insurance or all the other things that were under control.

The only effective way to manage the weekly cash back then was to hide and separate as much as possible. To do this, my mum had two purses – the white one that lived in the cupboard and the brown one that she carried with her. Each had multiple pockets, and every week she put enough in each pocket to cover the different expenses that would be coming up – one for the rates and electric, one for the coalman (yes, once or twice in the winter we'd get half a ton of coal delivered, which we used for the fire), and one for clothes, Christmas and holidays. Even the brown purse she carried with her had a back pocket for the milkman, newspapers and butcher, who all got paid weekly.

In principle, I grew up being good at budgeting, but with my dad's work ethic. I worked after school, on weekends and in the holidays, with my dad at first for free or a few pence a week, but by age 14 I was working at the local wildlife park on a massive £1.05/hour (around AU$2). From then on, I paid for all my own clothes, deodorant (a substance never before seen in the house) and records and saved up to travel to Germany and the US and go backpacking through Asia to Australia.

In 1989, aged 21, I met my wife, Kelly, who was the polar opposite of my mum when it came to finances. When we met in Sydney, where she grew up, Kelly was working two jobs while living back at home with her mum so she could save enough money to travel to Canada to see her boyfriend Mike. We've still not been to Canada.

But Kelly was hopeless with money. Not only was she spending all her income on cosmetics, clothes and jewellery and only ever drinking Chivas when she went out, she was also running up credit card and store card bills at David Jones. After a brief three weeks apart, while I backpacked through New Zealand, Kelly decided to travel around Australia with me.

As backpackers, we did it my way: hitchhiking was free, I had a two-man tent and we made our $50 daily budget cover everything, including site fees for the tent, food and entertainment. There were occasional arguments about whether or not we could afford the chocolate she wanted, but basically she trusted my judgement.

By this stage, we'd fallen in love and decided to let nature take its course and start a family. I'd resolved by age 19 that I wanted to be a young dad. I remember playing football in the back garden with my little siblings and thinking that their dad should be playing with them instead of getting home from work exhausted and having a sleep on the sofa. He had lots of energy with me in his twenties and thirties, but less for them in his forties.

Three weeks after our decision, our first son, Joshua, was on his way and we were still on backpacker incomes back in Sydney. Always a forward planner, I had a job lined up with Unilever back in the UK – a huge multinational that hired so many graduates that they let them take a year off before starting work. I'd already extended this to a second year off, but with Josh on the way I wrote and asked if I could come back part way through my second gap year to be a responsible parent.

The irresponsible, responsible parents

In the beginning, my salary of around £12,750 (AU$23,000) at Unilever was enough to cover most of our living costs, but it helped when Kelly worked part-time for a few weeks before our son arrived. I was paid monthly, with a three-week wait for the first salary deposit, so we got a credit card to cover the first weeks. Without realising, I had set us up in the worst way possible – everything on card, pay off the card when the salary lands, spend the leftover salary on stuff I can't even remember now, and repeat.

Within three years, my salary had doubled, our second son, Jack, was born in Brighton, England, and we'd moved back to Sydney, with me still only 25. I quickly rejoined Unilever in Sydney and, after a couple of years re-establishing myself, got back on the career ladder – because we all know the only way to start saving is to earn more, right?

Two years later, we managed to buy our first property, when we got moved up to Brisbane, using our credit card for the deposit. Two years after that, we sold it for a profit of <$10,000 after costs so that we could buy a home in Sydney, using our very meagre 5% deposit, funded by a generous relocation package from the company, because we were so terrible at saving.

Altogether I worked fifteen years for Unilever, leaving Australia for Bangkok after eleven of those years. For those first eleven years, we managed our finances the way most people do – one bank account, a credit card and one savings account. We were just as likely to use the savings account to take money back out to cover a bigger-than-normal credit card bill than to put money in and actually save.

It always seemed hard to save, especially with one, two, and then three kids. There were always reasons why we missed our savings goals this month, or this year – maternity leave, baby clothes, baby furniture, washing machine breakdown, more baby clothes, new TV, someone's wedding, toddler clothes, holiday, new kitchen, school uniforms, kids' clothes and did I mention clothes for us?

'There's too many clothes in the world.'
— Charlie Phelps, c. 1985

I thought we just needed more income, so I worked hard and got promoted, we took in foreign students, Kelly worked more hours, I got promoted again, and looked into Amway and other pyramid schemes. But no matter how much we earned, we always missed our savings goals.

The only time we had any success was with the envelope system – drawing out cash and putting it into different labelled envelopes and using them each for the appropriate purpose. But that was time consuming and circumstances changed again, so we reverted to paying everything on credit card, sweeping it in full when my monthly salary landed and repeating this month in, month out for over a decade.

Luckily for me, my next promotion was to Bangkok, where I was paid a relatively low local wage, plus a portion of my Australian salary was being paid into a separate account back in Australia. Suddenly we managed to survive on the local salary and it always seemed like too much hassle to move money from Australia to Thailand, so we simply saved the Australian salary. We saved more in each of those four years than we did in the previous eleven years combined.

From that time on, we always separated our money into different buckets – the money we were allowed to spend and the money that had to be set aside for more important things. Giving control of most of the spending money to Kelly allowed her the same freedom to spend that my dad used to have when he went to the pub. Once the important stuff is taken care of, it doesn't matter what the rest of the money is spent on and it's always a little hard to access more.

In the end, I learned as much about the psychology of money from Kelly, who loves to spend, and my dad, who knew he was no good with money, as I did from my very frugal mum, which is why I knew I was the right person to write this book.

A change of focus

After fifteen years, I was fed up with the corporate world and took a redundancy payment, which I used to fund two years in the UK as a trainee teacher and Newly Qualified Teacher, teaching high-school maths initially and later Economics and Business Studies.

I'd been inspired by Robert Kiyosaki's *Rich Dad, Poor Dad* and my love of Monopoly to focus on working at what I enjoyed and investing in property.

While in the UK, I used our savings to take advantage of the rapidly changing property market over there and bought three relatively cheap, cash positive investment properties. Then we moved back to Australia, where I found my UK teaching qualification unacceptable to the NSW Department of Education, so I decided to try my hand at mortgage broking – arranging home loans for commission.

As a broker, I suddenly got to see how hundreds of other people managed their money and quickly realised that:

- High income does not equal high savings

- Lower income does not equal low savings

In fact, there was almost no relationship between savings and income. There was, however, a strong correlation between bank account structure and income.

People on high incomes who manage their finances the way I did for eleven years were hopeless at saving unless the household was full of TAs like me, who never spend money, on anything, ever. People separating their finances out into different bank accounts, though, were much better savers, regardless of income.

It turned out that I was really good at mortgage broking and loved showing people how to invest in property. I also started to help people set up their bank accounts to be better at saving. I even went and got a diploma in financial planning so that I could sell advice on budgeting. It turns out that selling advice about budgeting isn't really what financial planners do, so I developed some tools and videos and just gave away the advice for free.

Along the way, our kids had grown up, and, not sure where we wanted to live, we sold the family home in Dulwich Hill and became 'rentvestors' – renting where we wanted to live and investing where the returns were strongest. We invested in the US market when it was at its lowest and the Australian dollar was worth the same as theirs, and also in Brisbane and the Sunshine Coast.

Since moving back to Australia in 2009, we have managed our money through the five-2 system explained in this book, although we have at least eight accounts spread across four banks. I manage the bills, a tiny everyday account for my $25/week pocket money, long-term savings and holidays. Kelly has an everyday account, a fun account and a savings account for Christmas and household appliances.

In that time, our income has gone from zero, while we built the business, to regular salaries, but we've only changed the amounts going through the spending accounts three times in 10 years. And that's one of the most important lessons to learn – when our income goes up every year with pay rises or promotions, unless we are actively managing our spending, the spending will simply grow to absorb the new income and we don't feel any better off.

Benefits of this book

This book will take you through the five Ps of financial success through property. The first of those, *Prepare*, is probably the most important part. In it, we talk about the minimum five bank accounts spread across two banks and covering our income. This sounds like a lot of accounts, but it gives us financial control. It also allows us to spend money guilt-free without worrying about whether it's going to mean a missed direct debit payment or impact our future or our ability to take a holiday.

I've coached couples through this, and then a year later asked how it's going. One couple just looked at each other and said, 'I guess we haven't argued about money for a year.'

The second stage, *Plan*, gets you to think about what you're going to do. People often go out and buy a place and they don't realise its only meeting a short-term need. There are five life stage needs if you have a partner and kids, or three without kids. It's important to understand which of those life stages you're buying for, because buying and selling is so expensive.

Then there's the *Purchase* process, where we'll help you understand how much you can really afford based on your goals and getting ahead.

Ideally, you can start building a *Portfolio* of properties. Buying a diverse range of different types of property in different locations so that you spread the risk. A local market may fall, but there are many different property markets that move independently of each other.

Once you build a portfolio, how do you *Pay Down* the debt and what do you do with the rest of your life?

My wife and I are in the very fortunate position of not having to work if we don't want to, and so we only do the work that makes each of us happy. Sharing what I know and helping other people get ahead does that for me. My wife, on the other hand, doesn't want to work more than a few hours a week. Her happiness comes from staying at home or spending time with friends or with our grandson. Who wouldn't want that freedom of choice?

Now let's figure out why it is that you need seven bank accounts to manage your money effectively. I know I said five earlier, but the reality is most couples end up with more. So good luck with it, and let's get on.

PREPARE

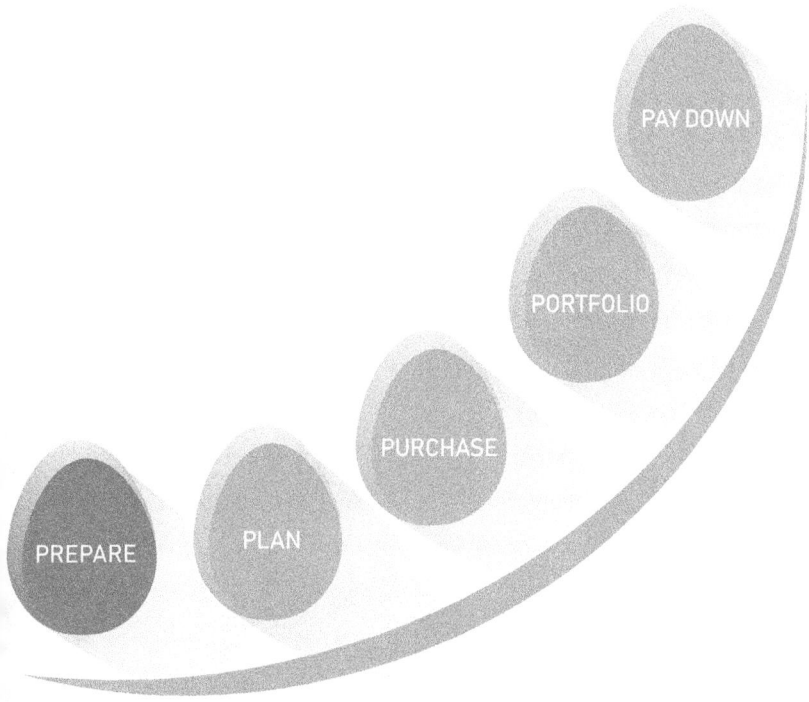

TWO

The Five-2 Money Diet

I'm assuming you're all grown-up now, and that you've got a job (or own a business) with great prospects, are paying bills and enjoying life, and even have some super holidays planned. But are you moving forward?

Sometimes there seems to be enough, and then other times things seem to get out of control:

- The car rego (road tax) falls due

- The electric bill is higher than expected

- The glass on your smartphone smashed and it was time for an upgrade anyway

- Christmas came around way too fast

- Who wouldn't love a new car

- Maybe you need to buy an expensive ring

- You're getting married

- You're putting some money aside for maternity leave

- You need to save for a house

It seems that the more we earn, the more we spend, and people will often blame the cost of living. This is normally an internal justification for a lack of understanding of what things cost and where the money goes. We think:

> 'There must be grown up way to manage all this stuff.'

> 'Maybe credit cards with an offset account are the answer.'

> 'Is there an app that can help me?'

> 'How about I plan a holiday to work it all out while I'm away and can come back refreshed?'

The problem is that we live in a cashless society, so it's just too hard to stay on top of everything when auto-payments and tap-and-go are so easy yet saving the deposit for a house seems so hard. We have become disconnected from our money when we spend.

In my experience, it's not income that determines spending but access to money.

The more money we can access, the more we spend.

For most people, the account they spend from is the account they are paid into, which simply means the more they earn, the more money they have access to.

The great news is, the five-2 system is a practical, common-sense solution that works *with* the technology and our own psychology, instead of trying to go off the grid. It lets us have the important elements of our lifestyle now and in the future, without being forced to work until we die.

I'm going to simplify the scary process of budgeting into a few steps anyone can implement straight away to instantly give them control of their life. I'm not going to suggest living in a shoebox, subsisting on baked beans and noodles, or tell you not to drive a Tesla if you want one. I'm just going to show you how to prioritise money for important things like food, shelter, stuff that makes you happy and your future.

Why so many separate accounts?

If you've got less than five bank accounts spread across at least two banks, managing money will be hard – except for the small percentage of us who are card-carrying TAs and who live alone or whose partners are also TAs.

First let's separate transactions into two categories: fixed and predictable versus variable:

Bills (fixed/predictable)	Everyday (variable)
Gas, electric, phone, internet, car insurance, car registration, health insurance, income protection insurance, etc.	Groceries, fruit and veg, lunches, coffees, takeaways, regular entertainment – basically anything you do every week
NO ATM/EFTPOS card	ATM/EFTPOS card

This means that anything in the everyday account is ok to spend, without worrying about what day direct debits come out, or when the next bills are due. Bills can bunch up throughout the year but are very predictable over the full year. Most people in couples end up with one everyday account each, to give them some autonomy and avoid confusion over who spent what and when.

Then we need to split our savings into a minimum of three accounts:

Future Freedom	Holiday (Annual)	Fun (Monthly)
To buy property and income-producing assets, for our future	To make memories, with awesome trips to see amazing sights and meet extraordinary people	Gifts, Clothes, toys, gadgets, mini-breaks, celebrations, beauty treatments, etc.

Remember this is the *minimum* we need – we might need another account to save for a car, for Christmas, for a wedding or for something else, but most people find it's best to do it separately to make the purpose clear. Most couples have a fun account each, but as a TA I don't need one.

Cash flows and timing to keep us on track

Having five accounts alone is not enough. It's the flow of money that makes the system stick:

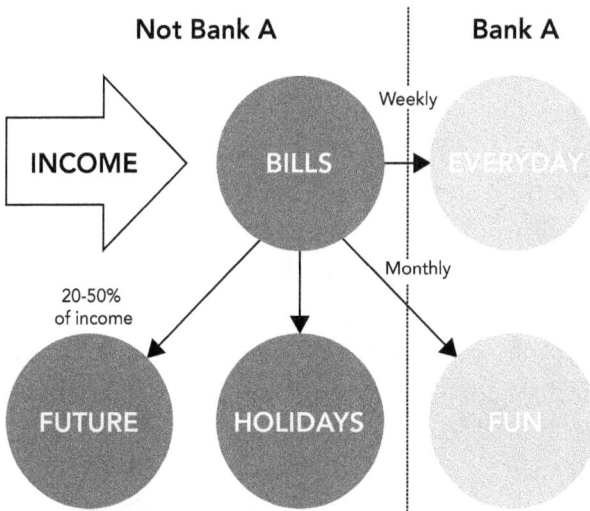

Fig. 2.1

But if you did all this with the same bank, how easy would it be to cheat?

We need to hide the important stuff away, so the everyday and fun accounts (light grey) can be with Bank A. The other three accounts (dark grey) can be with any other bank *except* bank A. For us, that's one bank to spend from and a different bank to cover our fixed expenses, holidays and savings.

Now that we have the salary flowing into the bills account, we can choose the timing of the automatic transfers to the other accounts.

Anyone that's ever been paid monthly knows that there's always too many weeks in a month and then there's the nightmare five-week months. People paid fortnightly know the pain of the no-pay week. We can fix that by putting money into the everyday account *weekly* – the same flat amount regardless of when we get paid and what the bills are for that week, fortnight or month. It's easy to cope for two to three days if the money runs out in a week, but not for a whole week of a fortnight, or the last two weeks of a month.

The fun account is a little different – *monthly* works best. It triggers our brains into thinking about birthdays and special events before we go blowing our allowance on other stuff that might need to wait until we have a quiet month. It also gives us a big enough lump to have some fun with, knowing the weekly allowance will still come if we spend it all at once.

When we explain this face to face with clients, we get a bunch of questions. What about credit cards? Shouldn't all the money be in my offset account? What if my income is uneven? How much should be in each account? What if our circumstances change? Which account should my rental income go into? Why don't they teach this in schools? We'll answer all these questions later in the book.

Saving for the World Cup

When I met with Dharmesh and Karen, they were renting and wanted to save for a house deposit, but they also wanted to enjoy going to live concerts regularly, take an annual trip home to India and – in two years' time – go to the World Cup. We went through their numbers in detail and prioritised funds.

	Yearly	Monthly
Income	**$108,000**	**$9,000**
Future	21,600	1,800
Hols India	2,000	167
Hols World Cup	7,500	625
Bills – Rent	26,000	2,167
Bills – Other	12,000	1,000
Fun – Concerts	4,800	400
Fun – Other	8,100	675
Everyday	26,000	2,167

For holidays, we averaged their $15,000 World Cup trip across the two years, in addition to their $2,000/year India trip, to make $9,500/year. The fun account had to cover gifts and similar expenses, plus $400 each month on concert tickets. Future savings were increased from $5,000/year to $20,000/year. Rent and other bills were covered, and then they each had a weekly allowance of $500 between them ($26,000/year), which unfortunately also had to include cigarettes.

One year after we implemented this plan, everything was on track. In fact, pay rises gave them a little more to play with, but they didn't want to increase the weekly allowance, putting more towards fun, holidays and the future instead. Two years later, and my check-in was more of a social call to chat about the World Cup and how easy managing money had become, plus how to use the holiday money for going to the Olympics in two years' time. Importantly, they'd both taken the decision to quit smoking, so we could rearrange things and save even more. Their bills also dropped with lower income insurance premiums for non-smokers.

Beautiful nails versus pizza

Traditional budgeting puts the emphasis on cutting things out, but the five-2 approach puts the control of what we buy firmly in our hands, and every person will choose to buy different things. When we first started the five-2 approach, Kelly suddenly started to have a weekly manicure, paid for out of our everyday account, which she managed for the family. (This is in the days before shellac, when nail polish only lasted a week.) That's right, Kelly was able to increase her weekly spending *after* we started budgeting. Her nails looked lovely and she felt good about herself, but come Friday night when me and the boys would ask to order pizza – a previous regular routine – Kelly told us there was pasta in the cupboard. All we wanted was a feed, so we made some spag bol instead and didn't mind at all. For Kelly, it was more important to spend $25 on getting her nails done than $40 on pizza. She knew we wouldn't care; and anyway, it's quicker to cook spag bol than to order and wait for pizza.

Everyone makes their own choices, given limited access to resources – in this case, money.

Credit cards suck!

One way to understand credit cards is to look back in time: 40 years ago, everything was done in cash and wages were normally weekly. You'd receive around $200 in your wallet each week. Anyone who walked around with that $200 on them was risking spending their rent money. But at least when you spent cash, you knew that money was coming out of your wallet. You could see it, touch it and know what was left over, relative to your pay.

Over time, we started to use bank accounts more, using cheques at first and then the miracle of debit cards. These days we're tapping and not really paying attention to the amounts that are being charged to our cards.

Credit cards complete the disconnect between money and spending. If you wind the clock back again 40 years, imagine if you were given $1,000 instead of $200. All you've earned is $200, but $1,000 is what you carry around on you, and you just hand out that money to buy stuff.

It's likely that the $1,000 is going to gradually disappear and your wage is just getting used to pay back the credit card. Credit cards give you access to money that you have *not yet earned*. A lot of people say that they are responsible with credit cards, that they always pay the bill in full and never pay interest. But it still means that every time they're making a purchase decision, it's not based on the money they have available or how much money they could and should be spending; they're just deciding they want it and then tapping and going. It's become normal behaviour to do that and the credit card never says 'no'.

I used a credit card 'responsibly' for eleven years, never paying interest and always paying in full every month. Yet every year for those eleven years, when I looked forward at the start of the year to what I could save versus when I looked back at what I actually did save there was about a $20,000 gap. That $20,000 gap over 11 years is $220,000. Thankfully I stopped that credit card use sixteen years ago, but that $220,000 sixteen years ago would be worth $450,000 now, if I'd put it in the share market, or about $1.1 million if I invested it into property. So, I'm $1.1 million poorer right now because I used my credit card 'responsibly'.

Please learn from my mistakes.

When we only use a debit card, the debit card will sometimes say 'no'. It'll say, 'Enough is enough, there's no more money left.' We then have a choice, either 'no, I don't want to buy that', or 'I need to buy that' and find money from somewhere. It's a conscious decision to take money from the fun, bills, holiday or future account *before* we buy, rather than sucking money out of those accounts six weeks later when a credit card bill is due.

Nowadays I only use a credit card to pay bills and to pay for holidays based on what I've got in my holiday account. I don't carry a credit card in my wallet. I do keep one in my car, though. When I go and tap something and my debit card says 'no', I can then say, 'I'll be back in a second, I've got my credit card in the car'. If it's something really important, I fetch it, and if not, I jump in my car and leave. This happened when I recently went to pay for a chiropractor's appointment, which I consider to be a bill, and it was slightly embarrassing for a few minutes, but I paid it so there was no issue.

There's nothing intrinsically wrong with credit cards, it's just as human beings we tend to spend what we can access, and credit cards give us too much access. When our little choices always get a 'yes' from the pay-wave machine, we don't realise we're taking money away from our future or a fantastic holiday. If we use the five-2 system, then credit cards are not necessary and can ruin a good plan.

Why not try it for a month? Take your credit card out of your wallet and leave it in the car, or at home. Unlink it from your phone, unlink it from your watch, and see how you feel and what happens to your spending. It's only a trial – and who knows, you could be the exception to the general principal and find your spending doesn't change at all.

Frequent flyers don't help

I know we can get frequent flyers for using our credit cards, but they are paid incentives designed to get us to spend more. They are not free. Every merchant is being charged 1–3% for us to use the card and often adding this to the cost. Using a credit card for all our spending is a bit like eating all our meals at an all-you-can-eat buffet. Some days we might be really good and not overeat, but if every meal was at a buffet, seven days a week, for a whole year, most of us would be struggling with a weight problem. Frequent flyers is a bit like getting free gym membership if you eat at the buffet every day – it balances out a little bit of the extra food we consume, but even after the extra workouts, we'd probably still be overweight. Let's look at the maths.

By putting everything on the card, instead of just bills and travel costs, it's possible to add around 20,000–40,000 points. Enough for one or two return flights from Sydney to Brisbane or Melbourne, which would normally cost $200–$400. That's the equivalent of $17–$34/month 'saving'. But what's the probability of getting a monthly credit card bill to be within $30 of what we would spend if we used a debit card? For most people, comparing what they spend on a credit card to what they would spend on a debit card, the gap will be hundreds, or even thousands, of dollars per month, not $20–$30.

Why not put a $50 allowance in the holiday or fun account for that flight, instead of giving up control of our finances and wasting thousands of dollars just to get it for 'free'?

How to accelerate savings

Once they are managing their money, some people might find they're not saving fast enough to get where they want to go. That could be because they're not earning enough money or because their lifestyle is actually a bit more expensive than they'd like it to be. Here are some simple steps you can take to help accelerate savings.

1. Move back home with parents or family, or move in with someone else to cut rent expenses. It's not something I'd recommend long term, but imagine you could save the deposit for a property three to five years quicker by living with family for a year? Someone paying $600 a week in rent can move home for a year and add $30,000 on top of their regular savings.

2. Increase income. Once our spending is under control, the more we earn, the more we save. Consider a second job or some extra shifts if your job allows. I wouldn't recommend working more until the money is under control, though. Otherwise, the more you earn, the more you spend, and you're not further ahead, just busier.

3. Work for a promotion. Asking talent scouts what we're worth to another company can give us a good idea of what's out there, but I don't recommend switching companies unless the current company or job is horrible. For people in a decent company or a decent job, peace of mind comes from where you are, and I place a lot of value on loyalty. I remember once being offered a 40% pay rise to leave Unilever and go to another company. The problem was, the other company that offered me the job was a local company and

there was going to be no opportunities to travel in the future. Instead I renegotiated my salary and got a small pay rise by offering to take on more responsibility at Unilever. I also spoke to the general manager, who gave me an indication that it was just a matter of time before I got promoted to the next level anyway. A promotion is a much better way to get a pay rise, because a better job with more responsibility beats switching companies and having to start all over again with local networks and friendship groups within a new company.

4. Some people start up a business in their spare time to prepare themselves for a more independent future. If you can find a way to make money quickly through that, fantastic. But be aware that businesses are often a drain on money in the first couple of years rather than putting money into our pockets.

Hitting your goals

Once we have a structure set up the way that we want it, we can set other goals that we might have. For example, a lot of people add another account just for Christmas if it's a big thing in their household. A couple of hundred dollars put aside each month between January and December means that we've got $2,500 to spend at Christmas.

Most of us would love a new car, and unless you're running your own business or doing a lot of work kilometres, getting a car through your employer may not be the best idea. Novated leases and other employer car benefits are typically based on borrowing to buy a newer, more expensive car than you would buy with your own money and the historical tax benefits have largely been eliminated. On the other hand, saving up for a car is an incredibly rewarding thing to do. An extra account labelled 'car' is a great idea. One of my clients has got a 'Tesla' account for his goal of buying a Tesla Model S. When he's got enough money in that account, he knows that, although it's a very expensive car, he can go out and spend that money guilt-free.

Other people plan to upgrade their furniture. My wife's been doing this for a long time. She has a spare account, and so she might, for example, put money aside for a few months from the fun account into the spare account. And then, once she's got enough money in the spare account, she'll go and buy a new TV or whatever she has set her sights on.

Holidays and travel are near and dear to my heart. I want people to take memorable holidays. Some of us have a 'normal' holiday every year and then a special holiday every few years. The normal holiday might be a couple of weeks a year somewhere not too far away. A special holiday might be a month-long trip to Europe or an African tour or attending an event like the World Cup. Knowing what those goals are, we can work backwards to see how long it's going to be before we go and how much we need to save.

To hit those savings goals, we spend in a controlled way instead of on a whim with a credit card and having to worry about the hangover later.

THREE

Protect Your Biggest Asset

How will you get paid if you're too sick to work?

People often think that their biggest asset is their home or their car, but for most people under 35 their biggest asset is their ability to earn an income. If we take a 25-year-old who's able to earn $100,000 or more per year, over a 40-year working life that's $4m. Income potential is dependent on education, the ability to get promoted, get paid and earn bonuses, and lots of other things, but the one factor that we all have in common is our health. Every year, many people are unable work for a period of time because of accident or illness. Sadly, some of them will be unable to work for years.

Protecting your biggest asset therefore means protecting your income. Some people already have income protection, either directly or in superannuation, but it's worth checking the amount of the cover and how long it lasts. A benefit period of at least thirty years (or to age sixty-five or seventy) would make sense. The worst coverage I saw, besides the countless people with $0 cover, was a 27-year-old earning $110,000/year who had cover inside super of $1,500/month for up to two years. That's a total of $18,000/year for two years, or $36,000 in total. His income capacity was around $4.4m and he wanted to borrow $600,000 for his first home, but he had only $36,000 in income insurance – we had to get that sorted fast.

Whenever I ask people how much of their income they would want to protect, they say '100%'. The maximum income protection insurance is normally 75% plus superannuation contributions. On $100,000/year, cover is $75,000 plus the $9,500 super = $84,500. Interestingly, this insurance can be held inside superannuation using a specialist insurance company, who, once a year, rolls money over to their dummy fund. The dummy fund pays the income insurance premium, to leave $0 balance. In the event of a claim, the benefit is paid to the dummy superannuation fund. When someone gets sick or injured and can't work for a while, they can draw down on superannuation depending on how long it's for and what else is going on.

Income insurance policies are not all equal, and a lot of insurance companies, insurance brokers or financial planners are afraid that people won't pay enough for long-term insurance. So, they sell the cheapest policy, which is called 'stepped premiums'. Stepped premiums are nice and cheap in your twenties and thirties, but every year the human body is more prone to wear and tear, illness and disease, so the insurance premiums go up as you get older. Through their forties and fifties, when a lot of people have still got young kids at home, big mortgages to pay, investment properties and a lot of debt, the premiums go up astronomically every year. By about age 47, after increases of 20–25% a year in the last few years, people cancel their insurances. Yet on average they still have 20 more years to work.

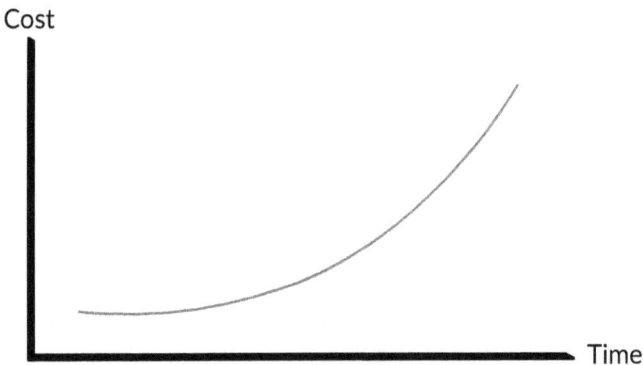

Cost

Time

Fig. 3.1 Stepped premiums

The alternative is to pay level premiums. This is like a contract with an insurance company to say, 'I'm 29, and I'm going to need insurance until I'm sixty-five. How much is that on average for the 36 years?' Once you make that commitment, the premiums are far lower over your working life. At first you pay the equivalent of stepped premiums of someone around ten to fourteen years older than you. Starting at 29, the premiums would be similar to those of a 43-year-old; but this means that when you're 50, you'll still be paying the premiums of a 43-year-old.

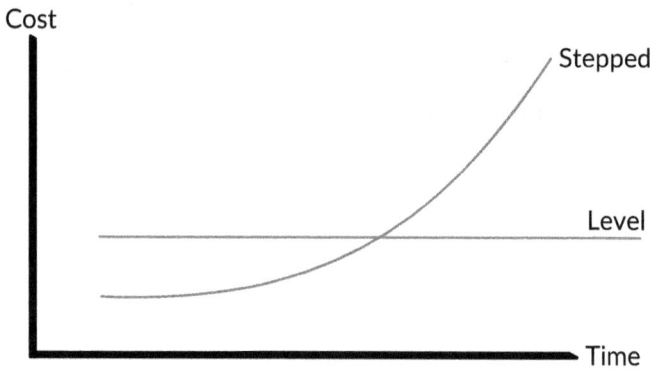

Fig 3.2 Level vs Stepped premiums

You might ask how paying an extra insurance cost is going to help you save up a deposit, but that's missing the point.

Do you insure your car? Is that car worth $4 million, or could you do that much damage to someone else's car in an accident? Imagine I gave you the keys for a

$4 million gold- and diamond-encrusted McLaren, to take for a spin. It's not insured, though, so if you put so much as a scratch on it, you have to pay for it out of your own pocket. How do you feel about taking that car for a spin around the block?

We need to get our incomes insured, make sure the premiums are level and make sure we cover ourselves to the maximum, ideally with an insurance company that does 'true level premiums'. It's getting a little bit technical, but let's say income this year for a 29-year-old is $100,000 and next year it might go up to $110,000. And it will keep growing each year. For most insurance companies, the first $100,000 would be level based on a 29-year-old. But the extra $10,000 would be level based on a 30-year-old. And the next $10,000 as a 31-year-old and the next $10,000 as a 32-year-old.

Alternately, a few insurance companies offer 'true level' cover where they increase cover at the same rate as your starting age. So, in our example, every extra $10,000 is assumed to be at the 29-year-old rate, even if the increase comes much later. An increase of about 20% per year is typically allowed, as if you had taken it at your starting age. Those companies can be a little bit more expensive in the beginning, but over 20 plus years the insurance premiums for someone on a career path will be way better. To find out more, get a quote from a financial adviser or an authorised personal protection representative, but be sure to ask for true level cover. If they don't know what that is, speak to someone else.

In my experience as a qualified financial planner, the only two times that stepped premiums made sense were for someone planning to move overseas within five years and a couple that had just quit smoking. Smoking increases premiums by over 50%, but to be classed as a non-smoker they needed 12 months without a cigarette. For them, we did stepped premiums in the first year and switched to level on renewal a year later.

So that's protecting 75% of earning potential. Next, we'll look at how to cover the other 25%.

Australia's under-insurance problem

Only around one in four Australians have income protection insurance, which is well below many other countries. A 2016 study across eleven countries by Zurich and Oxford University found that one of the main reasons for Australia's low rate is our optimism and false assumption that the risks are low. Below we can see that our insurance levels are lower than the 11-country average and significantly behind those of the US.

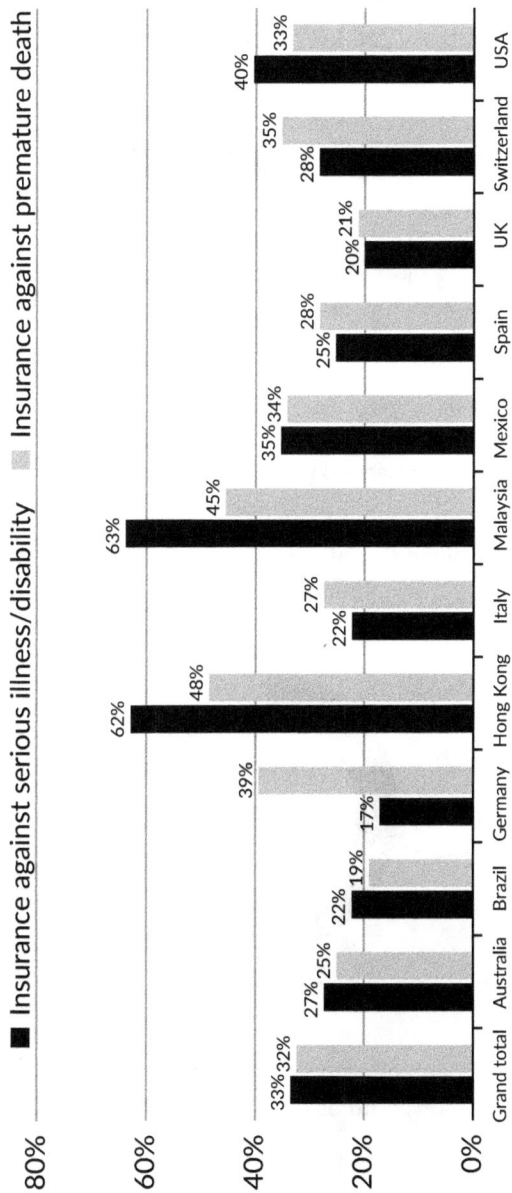

Fig. 3.3 Penetration of income protection insurance varies considerably

Source: Zurich/Smith School, University of Oxford, 2016

Base: Total n=11,584

Almost half of us think the risks of income loss due to accident or injury are less than 10%, whereas the correct figure is 44%.

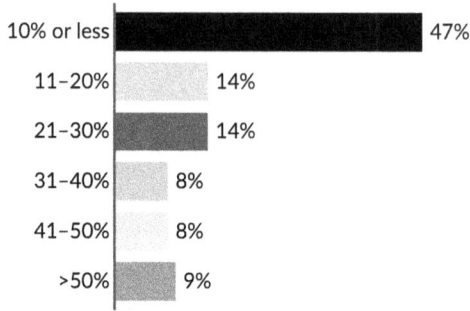

Base: working community n=1031

FIG. 3.4 Perceived risk of experiencing income loss due to illness/disability

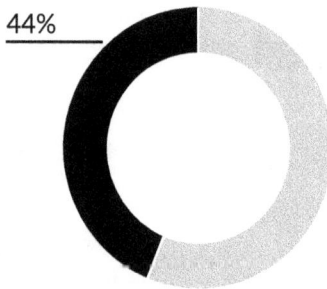

Base: working community n=1031

Fig. 3.5 Percentage who experience lost income due to illness/disability

The question is, if you knew there was a 44% chance of experiencing a loss of income due to illness or injury during your working life, would you buy insurance to cover that risk?

There are also false perceptions around the level of cover offered by worker's compensation, employers and government. Sure, work accidents are covered by work cover insurance, but anyone who's had to make a claim knows that they never seem to cover as much as we thought. Work cover doesn't provide any support for illness or any non-work-related injuries. Unlike Germany and some other North European countries, our government sets very low levels of income supplement and high barriers to claim. Average wages are around $80,000/year, but income support is only around $15,000/year and only kicks in after all your savings and other liquid assets have dropped below $5,500.

What if you couldn't work again?

In a real nightmare scenario, what if someone is never able to work again; for example, if they are badly injured in an accident? They would be totally reliant on income insurance and guaranteed to be 25% short of what they would have earned if they hadn't got sick or injured. This can be covered with *total permanent disablement*, or TPD, insurance. If you will never ever work again, you will be paid a lump sum, tax free.

Whether you use this lump sum to buy assets or pay off your house or put it into a savings account is up to you.

'TPD insurance' is defined in a few different ways. The best definition covers your *own occupation*. Even if you could take a lesser position after the illness / injury, in the same industry that you're with, it will still pay the same lump sum you would have received if you had to stop working altogether. The classic example used is a surgeon. If she mangles her hands in an accident, she can now no longer operate but is still a fully qualified doctor. The income she'd receive as a general practitioner or other type of doctor would be significantly lower than what it would be as a surgeon, so TPD 'own occupation' insurance would actually pay her out. Previously in my job as a mobile mortgage broker, I took out 'own occupation' TPD. If I had become unable to visit people in their homes because I couldn't drive, my ability to earn an income would have been lower.

The second TPD definition, which is the one that sits in most people's superannuation funds because it meets the condition of release of a superfund, is *any occupation*. This means someone will never work again in any occupation for which they are suitably trained and qualified. If they've done a number of jobs over the last five to eight years then got badly injured, but could go back to one of the jobs that they've done in the past, they wouldn't be able to claim. If an IT consultant was never going to work in IT again but could push trolleys in Woollies, that's not an occupation that they're trained and qualified for, so a normal 'any occupation' TPD policy would pay out.

The next definition was invented by one of the industry superfunds. They still call it 'any occupation', but it's any occupation for which you could be trained, not anything you currently do. So, if you could be trained to push the trolleys in Woollies, then they won't pay you out under their 'any occupation' definition.

It's important to be really careful about the definition of 'TPD' in any insurance policy.

There is another definition below all others: 'activities of daily living'. People don't normally choose to take out that kind of cover, but in certain circumstances, like having a highly risky job or some pre-existing conditions, it may be the only TPD cover available. This type of cover pays out for someone so badly injured, or ill, that they will need assistance in daily living, either to dress themselves, to bathe, feed, get out of bed, or go to the bathroom.

Another reason people take out TPD insurance is to be able to pay for care while their partner or family work, if the worst came to the worst.

TPD is a hugely important insurance to have. The amount is up to each person, but it's typically around

25% of their lifetime income, or a lump sum to provide an income or reduce costs (like debt).

TPD can be paid for and held inside or outside of super. TPD inside of super could be with a different company from the one where superannuation is held, similar to income insurance. Paying for TPD out of net income means earning money, paying tax and then paying insurance premiums. Paying through super is actually tax deductible to the fund because it's meeting some of the needs of the superannuation fund.

For example, suppose the annual premium was $1,000. 'Outside of super' means we've typically got to earn $1,500–$1,600 and then pay $500–$600 in tax to have $1,000. Paying through super, we only have to earn $1,000, which we can salary sacrifice. It's taxed at 15% on the way into the superfund, reducing it to $850. But then our superfund gets 15% tax relief on the insurance premium, so it only pays $850 to get $1,000 in cover.

There are certain benefits like 'own occupation' that can't be done through superannuation, but most companies these days will let us link the two policies together – part inside super and part outside super. Around 2/3 of the premium is inside super and 1/3 is outside super. In the event of a claim, the company looks and sees which definition it meets; if it meets the 'in super' definition, they pay the claim through super, and if it meets the 'outside super' definition, they pay directly. Again, talk to a qualified financial planner or someone who's licensed to sell insurance. TPD can be stepped or level, but typically level is going to be more economical over the long run. Alternatively it could be stepped, because as we go through life and build up assets, our need for the insurance may reduce over time.

How survivors get support

Letting the family live on is a gentle way of recognising that we're not on this planet forever. At some point we're going to die, and there's a risk that it might happen before we're ready. Single people often assume their families and loved ones can take care of themselves. But if you're in a relationship or plan to be, and have commitments, you need to make sure that your partner is taken care of. It's going to be enough of a nightmare for them to lose someone without having the financial problems that can be associated with that.

Life insurance covers this, and it's normally held inside super. When we ask people about the kind of things they want to cover, like paying off a mortgage, providing additional income for their partner and paying for the kid's education, we often end up with a figure of $1m or more. If the amount that's in superannuation isn't enough, then it's possible to just get the extra. For example, if a marketing consultant has $300,000 cover in super and she wants $1m, she can take $700,000 elsewhere. She can still hold this insurance inside a superannuation dummy fund, and can pay these premiums at level rates instead of stepped ones.

The difference between life insurance and income protection is that, as we build up assets and pay off debt, our need for life insurance tends to drop over time. This is the one insurance where I would say that it's worth looking at stepped cover versus level, and who the insurer is matters less. A death certificate or terminal illness diagnosis is not something even a dodgy insurance company can deny. Fortunately, life insurance also pays out in the event of terminal illness. We can potentially collect the life insurance early and use that to enjoy the rest of our days and know that the family is going to be okay, before we go. It's a horrible subject, but one worth thinking about for long enough to get the insurance cover, and then we can forget about it and not worry.

Beat cancer financially

The last of the insurances that we'll cover is the least well known, but I think it's one of the most important; for me, it's second after income insurance. If someone is not earning an income, I would still prefer that they've got this insurance in place. It's called trauma or critical illness insurance, and it pays a lump sum on diagnosis of something really horrible. This includes heart disease, stroke and cancer (read the insurer's product disclosure statement for the full list). For people under the age of 40, the majority of claims paid are for cancer, but this is not just a slight skin lesion the doctor will have off in five minutes. Claims are paid when cancer has become a bit more serious at stage three.

A cancer patient hopes that they can beat the disease with a combination of treatments and therapy. But treatments that they might need could be experimental, like a new drug not covered by Medicare or their health fund. They want to make sure that they've got the money to do whatever it takes to get fit and well again, which this cover provides. The other side to this equation is, for those in a relationship, with kids or even living with family, what about the loved one who wants to take time off work while the patient recovers? In that case, the fit and healthy person can't claim on their income insurance. Even though my wife is retired, we have trauma cover for her, so if something bad happens to her we'll get $220,000 paid as a lump sum. This would cover potential treatments and any drop in income or additional staff costs if I stop working to be by her side.

Because it's a no-strings-attached lump sum, trauma cover also enables you to take time to not be rushed back to work. Sometimes people need to take a career break. Imagine the psychological impact of a trauma event. Would you want to rush back to the same day job, or take that African safari first?

Like with any insurance, we hope we never make a claim, but trauma cover has the highest probability of claiming within your working life. It makes more sense that this one should be level and not stepped, so you can afford the cover into your forties and fifties when the risks rise dramatically. The great thing is, it's money to sort out a problem and then hopefully carry on with our lives. If it does go the other way, then life insurance can be linked to it.

Fundraisers versus insurance

A couple of years ago, my sister-in-law shared a link on Facebook promoting a fundraiser for a friend of hers. Her friend's husband was battling cancer and they desperately needed to raise around $100,000 to cover treatments, care and mounting bills due to lost income. Since then, we've had three invites to similar events or been sent links to GoFundMe pages, all looking for similar help. It's awful for them, but it's also not pleasant for us having to decide to go, or not go, to donate, or not, or figure out how much we can spare to help them. Is one friend worth $1,000 and another worth $100? Is $10 for a friend of a friend worth donating? All of these people could have had insurance to help them out of their difficult situations, but they either didn't know the insurance existed, or knew but didn't take it out.

Imagine someone having a car accident and causing $100,000 worth of damage to a Ferrari when they weren't insured. If they tried hosting a fundraiser, or a GoFundMe page to raise the funds, they wouldn't get any sympathy. They'd probably be trolled and ridiculed for not paying for insurance.

Obviously, we can be a lot more compassionate with illness or injury than car accidents, but I choose to buy the insurance in case something happens to Kelly or me. Apart from anything else, imagine the stress of organising an event and trying to put on a brave face, while your partner is fighting for their life.

Buffering for short-term income hits

A buffer is a fantastic way to get around short-term financial problems. It worries me when people buy a property and use every cent they've got in order to try and reduce their mortgage and mortgage insurance. The problem is that if anything happens, like unexpected repairs, pregnancy or sudden job loss, they won't have the funds to cope. A house is not like having a car, where it might cost $500 to get it fixed. With a property it can cost tens of thousands of dollars to correct a problem.

Some of the insurances that we spoke about, like income insurance, typically have lower premiums if we take a longer wait period. For example, if someone has enough savings to cover themselves for three months, then they can pay a much lower premium. I recommend having enough funds to cover around three months of expenses as a buffer.

Stage One: Prepare summary

Before you start rushing out to buy a property, we need to make sure you're properly prepared.

1. Sort out your money management system to make you great at saving and paying down debt, while being able to enjoy your life. After three months of the five-2 system, it'll feel normal.

2. Buy as much income protection as you can afford and cover other gaps with TPD and life insurance.

Buying property without these two preparations in place is significantly riskier than having your shit together first.

PLAN

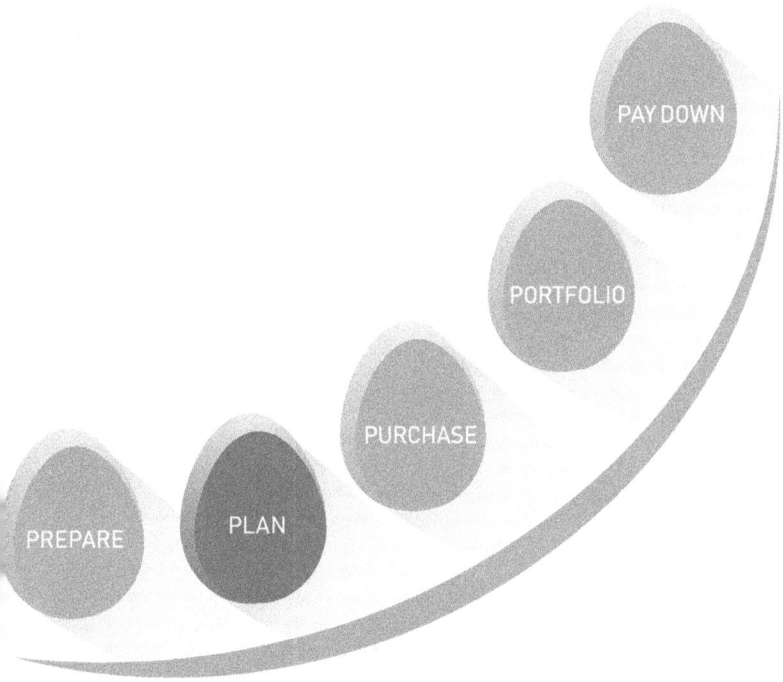

PAY DOWN

PORTFOLIO

PURCHASE

PREPARE

PLAN

FOUR

Life Stages Plan

The five life stages and your changing property needs

Often when I sit down with people and look at where they want to go, they say they want to buy a place to get into the market. What they don't consider is that there are five separate life stages if they have children, or three if they don't.

The five stages are set out in the table below, but they are very simple to explain with the example of Andrew, a young doctor.

Stage 1 – single. Maybe a one-bedroom or a studio is fine for Andrew. It's a perfect first purchase. It meets his short-term needs and it seems great all around.

Then he meets Zoe, a graduate sales manager. After dating for a while, they decide to move in together but quickly start to feel a bit claustrophobic.

Stage 2 – couple. Like most couples, Andrew and Zoe find a two-bedroom apartment, and it's wonderful. They have a home office which doubles as a spare room for when Zoe's family visit from Europe. Before too long, they decide to start a family and the two-bedroom place is perfectly fine for baby Jack, until he learns to walk...

Stage 3 – young family. All of a sudden, Jack is learning to walk and a backyard becomes a priority. Andrew and Zoe are trying for a second child, find they have one on the way and the urgency to get a place with a little backyard intensifies. They buy a nice little three-bedroom, one-bathroom terrace with a nice little backyard for Jack and Amy to play together in. Andrew and Zoe are happily settled in their family home until Jack turns eleven. He and Amy have stopped using the small backyard, which seems like a bit of a waste of space. They really need to be near a decent high school, near a park the kids can play in and somewhere with a second bathroom.

Stage 4 – mature family. When Jack and Amy are around 11–13, hormones are kicking in and they are not going to bed at 7:30 anymore. The family now looks for a place that's got a second living area and they absolutely need a second bathroom. Amy seems to hog the one bathroom they currently have, and Zoe hates to share it with Jack, who leaves the seat up and all kinds of mess. They upgrade to four-bedroom, two-bathroom house, over two levels, with two living spaces and a bit of separation and privacy from one another. Finally, they have their forever home and feel settled.

Stage 5 – empty nesters. Jack left home at twenty-one, but Amy held on until she was twenty-two and then went to London with some friends for a two-year working holiday trip. In the meantime, all those years of netball are making the stairs more of a challenge for Zoe's knees. The house is too big and they are going to have to downsize. This is where Kelly and I got to in our mid-forties. My knees were pretty well shot from football, and Kelly had early onset arthritis. We went for an apartment with a lift in the building.

Similarly, all of a sudden Andrew and Zoe are looking for a single-level home. They still want two bathrooms and three bedrooms for when Amy comes back from overseas or Jack comes to visit. Zoe uses one of the rooms as a home office, but it has a sofa bed in case everyone is home for Christmas. Finally, they are in a home forever, or at least until they move into a nursing home – that can be considered stage six, but we won't discuss it here since it usually doesn't involve buying property.

In this example of the five stages, Andrew and Zoe bought and sold at every stage. It's easy to understand how foolish it would be to do this in Australia where we have stamp duty on every purchase. They also had to pay a selling agent to sell each one. On average, you lose about 7% of the value of a property buying and selling.

A lot of people assume that property prices increase, which will cover the cost, but this may or may not be true. The table below shows some of the costs and consequences of going through those five life stages.

Family	Single	Couple +/- Baby	Family Young kids	Family Bigger kids	Empty nesters
Property needs	1 bed	2 beds	3 beds	3-4 Beds	2-3 beds
	1 bath	1-2 baths	1 bath	2 baths	2 baths
			Back yard	2 living	1 level
Sydney's Inner West	$600k	$800k	$1.2m	$1.8m	$1m
Buy/sell cost	$38k	$50k	$75k	$120k	$62k

For completeness, the table below is a guide for those without kids. The mature couple stage can kick in at a younger age but often involves a better-quality property, with a nicer outlook. Pets are more often a consideration for couples without kids.

Family	Single	Couple	Mature couple
	1 bed	2 beds	2-3 beds
Property needs	1 bath	1-2 baths	2 baths
			1 level
Inner West	$600k	$800k	$1m
Buy/sell cost	$38k	$50k	$62k

Costs and consequences of not thinking ahead

The biggest risk of buying property is the possibility of prices falling. Over the long run, prices have generally risen, but statistics tell us over the short run – say, two to four years – that they can fall. In Sydney right now, prices have been falling for around 18 months and seem set to fall further. The problem is the timeframe with any given life stage. Andrew and Zoe were only in their studio for two years and the two-bedroom apartment for four years. The houses lasted around 10 years each. Most people don't think beyond five years, which in property terms is actually quite short.

The first big costs are the buy costs, of around 5% of the value of the property. If you're lucky enough to get the first homeowners grant or stamp duty concession, fantastic. There are still legal fees, mortgage registrations fees, title registration fees, building inspections and other bank fees, currently around $4,000 on top of stamp duty. Selling agents typically cost around 2%

when it's time to sell, then there's a solicitor again, and discharge fees to the bank and to the state government. On a $600,000 property, it would cost around $15,000 to sell.

If Andrew bought his first property for $600,000 between the buy-in and get-out stage, he'd be up for around about $40,000 in costs. If he only owned the property for two years, that's $20,000/year. If he got lucky and the price went up 10% in two years, that's $60,000, leaving him only $20,000 ahead of where he started.

Buying a two-bedroom apartment for $800,000, Andrew and Zoe would be up for about $60,000 in costs, or around $15,000/year for the four years they owned it. Thankfully, there are better ways to do things.

Alternative strategies to win the long game

My favourite alternative strategy is to buy a future investment that you're going to live in temporarily. We know that it's just a temporary place, so we might compromise on where it is and on the size of the property, because the goal here is to get ahead. Andrew and Zoe could have kept the first property as an investment and rented a two-bedroom place until they were ready to buy a more sizeable family home to live in. In the meantime, they could have built up an offset account as the deposit for their next property.

The second strategy I really love, and it works really well in conjunction with the first, is to buy ahead of the curve. Andrew and Zoe could have bought a three-bedroom home with a little backyard as an investment property while they were still living in the studio or renting out a two-bedder. They could have taken advantage of any negative gearing benefits and used the higher rent on the three-bedroom place to cover the rent on a two-bedder. They could have had four years of paying down the bigger place until they were ready to move in. By not buying the two-bedroom place, they could have saved $60,000 in costs and got the benefit of any capital growth on the bigger property. Capital losses are less of an issue for a long-term family home, as long as the debt is manageable, so owners can pay it off in 10–15 years.

The third strategy is to buy a place that's expandable. For example, Andrew and Zoe could have bought a three-bedroom, one-bathroom home with flexibility to extend upwards or outwards, adding an extra living space, bathroom and bedroom when Jack and Amy got to high-school age. If the renovations were done well to keep a bedroom and bathroom downstairs, it would have also met their stage-five needs, when stairs are an issue.

The other strategy, which I employ, is renting where you want to live and investing where it makes sense to invest. This is sometimes called 'rentvesting'. We rented in the types of property we needed as our needs changed, in great locations which also have very low rental yield. We then invested for long-term capital growth or income, or a combination of both. The downside with this strategy is having to move if the landlord sells or wants to move back in. To combat this, we always sign a two-year lease to have a bit of stability. By asking for a two-year lease, a long-term landlord will think we're awesome, but a short-term landlord won't be interested in taking us on as tenants. Better to find that out at the beginning rather than when we've been in there for a year and then getting kicked out.

A 'getting it right' story

Now one of my favourite couples that I've worked with is David and Ellie. When I first met them, David was an accountant earning about $80,000 a year at the time, eight or nine years ago. Ellie was working as a junior marketing assistant and she was probably earning about $50,000. They were doing okay, but they were young, on a career path and looking to buy their first home together. At that stage they weren't even married. They were looking to buy a nice little terrace house in Summer Hill. I asked why and they said they wanted something to start a family in. We talked about the costs and consequences of stretching themselves to get into that little terrace house and how limited they were going to be in the long term. They also realised that they really wanted to live somewhere more central and so they bought a much cheaper apartment in Glebe instead. It was easier for them to afford it with the deposit that they had. Their mortgage was far more manageable than it would have been. They also knew it was going to be a long-term investment property.

Ellie and David bought it with an interest-only loan plus an offset and put all their savings into it. Four years later, they were married and their mortgage was costing them next to nothing. Their incomes had increased dramatically and they could afford to buy a lovely property with three bedrooms and one bathroom that was expandable in the future, but they rented it out and carried on living in Glebe. Two years after that, their first baby is almost a year old and they are just moving into their house. When they move in, they'll transfer all of their offset savings across to the family home and have a much smaller, more manageable mortgage plus be able to tax deduct their original mortgage on the Glebe unit, which will become their long-term investment.

David and Ellie have done a fantastic job of managing their life stages, and they're a lovely couple to boot. The big lesson from understanding the five life stages is to buy strategically for the long term, like David and Ellie, not tactically, like Andrew and Zoe.

FIVE

Home Or Investment

Why I love renting my home

I'm often asked, 'Should I buy a home to live in, or am I better off just investing?' The answer to that question is always very complicated, but let me just give you a little bit of my own story. We had a family home, a house that was big enough for all of us, in Dulwich Hill. But we lived overseas for a while. We came back again and the place was okay for our needs, but it only had one bathroom, which was becoming a strain with teenage boys in the household. Our oldest son was planning to move away from home to pursue his career. Our middle son was always going to move away from home quite young, based on personality. That would leave us with one at home. It didn't make sense to upgrade to meet our needs, but we also weren't ready to downsize to something to meet our future needs. Instead, we sold our home in Dulwich Hill.

This was in 2010, and anyone who knows the Sydney market since 2010 would think we were crazy. From 2013 to 2017, Sydney housing prices jumped 60–80% yet we got out of the market and began renting. Initially we were in a slightly bigger home with two bathrooms, two living spaces and enough bedrooms for all the boys. We tried living in a different area as well to test where we thought we could end up. A few years later, Kelly was starting to suffer from early onset arthritis in her knees. We moved to an apartment with great water, harbour bridge and city views, but by then we only had one son at home.

Apart from our changing needs, we chose to rent because the kind of property that we want to live in is really expensive to buy, yet not that expensive to rent. Rental yield, which is annual rent divided by property value, is only around 2.6% where we live, equivalent to $500/week on a $1m property. Annual strata, insurance, council rates and water rates cost around 1% of the property value, equivalent to $200/week on a $1m property. Worse still is that the market in Sydney is currently falling, due to the massive rises leading up to 2017.

When we sold our house in 2010, we put some of the proceeds into property in Phoenix, Arizona, when their market was at rock bottom after the global financial crisis. House prices there have predictably tripled since then, yet rental yields are still over 10%. Our US properties more than cover our Australian rent, but with much less risk.

Why bother owning a property at all?

Rents are likely to go up over time with inflation and increases in income, whereas the amount we borrow is fixed at the time we buy. We'd rather have the rent we're collecting going up at the same time as the rent we're paying does. Better that than not being in the market at all and finding that rent goes up indefinitely.

Every person's situation is different, so best to consider your situation, where you'd like to live and where you can afford to live, and work out the costs and risks of owning or renting. Importantly, determine how quickly you can reduce the debt on the property that you're living in. A good money coach should be able to help.

Short-term homes versus forever homes

What we saw with the life stages is that most homes people buy to live in are short-term homes until they buy a forever home. Why get hung up emotionally about a place that you're only going to live in for a few years?

I want to focus on the idea that your first and possibly second properties are short-term homes. How long will your first home meet your needs? We can then calculate the difference in costs between living in that property versus renting it. Depending on how much rent you would be paying if you were living in a rental property versus the rental return that you would get on an investment property, it may or may not be a good idea to move in. That would obviously be coupled with first home buyer benefits if they're available in the price bracket that you're looking at. Georgina, a research scientist, bought her first home while she was still happily living with her parents. She got a $20,000 stamp duty exemption by living in the place for six months and then moved back home and rented it out.

Let's look at the costs of living in versus renting out.

Weekly $	Renting	Own to live in	Invest
Rent	500	0	5UU
Mortgage interest	0	450	450
Other costs	0	100	100
Total/week	500	550	-50
Tax back	0	0	19
Net cost	500	550	-31

If rent is $500 a week, then that's all you pay. When you buy a property to live in, you pay interest on the mortgage plus council rates, water rates, strata, insurance, and any repairs and maintenance. We only take into account the mortgage interest, even if you have a principal interest repayment of, say, $650 a week. The interest cost of that loan might only be $450 a week, so the $650 repayment is $450 interest plus $200 off the principal. We find an average unit in Sydney has costs of $100–$150 a week in addition to the mortgage. The rent of $500 a week is therefore comparable to $550 in property costs to own. If the property was an investment, that $50 difference provides a tax deduction of around $2,600 a year. For someone earning over $90,000, that means about $1,000 tax back, or $19/week. It can therefore be cheaper to own a property and rent it out for $500/week and pay $500/week rent on another property. In this example, living in your own place would cost $550/week, but renting one and renting out another would cost $531.

On the other hand, if you're paying higher rent – say, $600 – then moving into a place with a mortgage that you can overpay may be much better. For example, you might find that the $450-a-week interest costs that we mentioned before very quickly drops to $420 to $400 to $380 as the loan balance is reduced.

Of course, if the alternative for you is living at home rent free with family, then either renting or paying a mortgage will seem very expensive and make you worse off in the long run. If living at home for longer is going to result in a domestic homicide, however, then that might not be best for your long-term future. Maybe setting a goal for moving out – for example, when the interest cost is below \$400/week – would give both an incentive to increase repayments and an end point to living with your family that's manageable.

In summary, when looking at the cost of moving into a property, we have to firstly think of it as a temporary residence rather than a forever home. Secondly, we weigh that up against the cost and benefits of renting elsewhere and getting tax deductions.

Investing strategies to suit your needs

I'm a long-term investor and there are a number of investment strategies I've tried and looked into, and lots of clients I've helped with different strategies. The weakest investment strategy that you can ever come up with is to invest for the tax benefits. It means buying something that loses money to claim back some of that loss from the government. We'll look at negative gearing in the next section.

Some investment strategies worth looking at are: cash flow, capital growth and forced value.

In certain areas, at certain times, we get a better yield than in other areas, and its possible for a property to be cash positive after paying the mortgage interest and other costs. There's often a trade-off between yield and capital growth. The yield is a comparison with bank interest.

Paying $500 per week rent on a $500,000 property amounts to $26,000 per year, which is a 5.2% yield ($26,000/500,000). Anything below a dollar per thousand, like $500/week for a $500,000 property, will be less than 5%. Investment mortgage rates are currently around 4.5%, so it might be possible for that property to be neutrally geared or cash flow positive. If the cost of funds is 4.5% and there are 0.5% costs in agent fees, rates, strata, etc., then a 5% yield could be enough to break even. A 5.5%, 6% or 7% yield would be cash positive.

One way to achieve cash positive status is to buy a property below market value; the property could be worth $500,000, but you pay $450,000 and still collect $500 a week in rent. Amazingly, most people don't try this and simply pay the market price without attempting to pay less.

There are other tricks, too, like a dual key, such as a house with a granny flat or a house with an apartment over the garage, or two houses on one lot. Suddenly we're collecting two lots of rent and yield is significantly higher, and therefore it's a cash flow positive property. It's also possible to do this with a single house. Instead of renting the whole house, each room can be rented separately, or the house can be split into two separate rentable dwellings.

Cash flow is one investment strategy, but an area where yields always seem good often means the capital growth is not so good.

Over the long run, capital growth will beat a pure yield strategy. For example, Carolyn, an HR manager, could buy for $500,000. She looked at Bathurst, which tends to have very low capital growth and also very low rental growth. The yield of $500/week rent seemed good, but in five years' time she might still only collect $500. By contrast, a place in a much better area closer to a city with lower rent – say, of $400 a week – might get $500 or higher five years later because of the demand for rentals. Carolyn realised that although the yield would be lower for the first five years, her property was more likely to grow in value. A $500,000 property in Bathurst would be worth around $500,000–$520,000 in five years' time, whereas the city property could be worth $650,000 by then. Having $150,000 as a capital gain is significantly better than the difference in rent each year.

We can't assume that just because the value of an area has gone up for the last five or 10 years it's going to carry on that way. History tells us it's not true, and right now Sydney and Melbourne are experiencing their biggest fall since 1983. When we're looking at capital growth, we need to look at long-term trends and the fundamentals that are in that market, like population growth, employment growth and restrictions on land. Population growth and employment growth in an area with lots of land, which is the case in many rural towns in Australia, will mean people will just cut up another block of land and put another house on it. Real estate is only going to grow in those areas because the cost of building grows, which is in line with inflation.

The third strategy I want to mention is sometimes called forced value or subdivisions. It involves buying a place on a big block (800–1,000 square metres) and carving off a piece of land to either sell or put another dwelling on. Suddenly we've got two houses where there was only one, or two incomes where there was only one. It's possible to make a lot of money very quickly by doing this. But it is much riskier, more complicated and we need a lot more experts around us. People like town planners, architects, building surveyors and obviously a good builder to make sure that what we're doing is going to make money, not just eat up time and energy. If we get it right, then there's a lot of money to be made in real estate with smaller subdivisions or bigger lot subdivisions.

Having said that, I think subdivisions would be a bad idea for your first investment property. We try and show people how to get used to buying and holding property before trying something more complex. The emotional rollercoaster that comes with owning property becomes more manageable when you've done it once or twice.

There are lots of other little niches that can work for people, but the three main ones are cash flow positive properties, capital growth properties and smaller subdivisions.

Is negative gearing worth it?

Negative gearing is very peculiar to Australia and doesn't exist in other parts of the world. First, let's understand the difference between getting a tax deduction and negative gearing.

Let's look at two scenarios, shown in the table below.

	Positive	Negative
Rent	+30,000	+25,000
Mortgage interest	-20,000	-25,000
Agent and other costs	-5,000	-5,000
Taxable	+5,000	-5,000

In the positive scenario we collect $30,000/year in rent. If mortgage interest costs are $20,000, and agent fees, rates and insurances are around $5,000, that's

$25,000 in costs. These are tax deductible. This means instead of paying tax on the $30,000 rent, we only pay tax on the $5,000 profit. In the second scenario, rent is only $25,000/year and interest costs are also $25,000. Now we're paying $30,000 in costs including rates and insurance and losing $5,000 per year. This is called negative gearing. It means we've borrowed so much money and are paying so much in interest that we're actually making a loss. Under current legislation, someone earning a salary of $100,000 a year would claim back the $5,000 from their investment property and only pay tax on $95,000. They would probably get around $2,000 back in tax. It sounds great if we're the ones getting the $2,000 tax refund but is inherently unfair on the 90% of people that don't negatively gear.

Imagine three work colleagues each earning $100,000: Alex, Ben and Caitlyn. Alex has no other investments, so pays tax on their $100,000 income. Ben has a part-time business through a company he started, which is currently losing $5,000 per year. He won't get any tax breaks on that loss, but if he makes $5,000 profit on the business next year, he won't pay tax on that. The loss is carried forward to offset against future gains. Caitlyn buys an investment property which loses $5,000 per year, declares that loss in her tax return and gets $1,950 back. All three earned $100,000, but Caitlyn pays less tax because she chose to buy a loss-making investment. Both Ben and Caitlyn expect to make a profit in the future, but the ATO (Australian Taxation Office) subsidises Caitlyn's loss and not Ben's.

When we buy a property that's in a good location with good potential for capital growth, we might be happy to make a short-term loss. Negative gearing is normal in Sydney for most properties and is very often the case on houses in Australian cities. In the long run, hopefully the property value and rents increase.

Negative gearing doesn't work when we're just losing money, getting a tax deduction to reduce the loss but not getting enough capital growth to offset that. In the example earlier, Caitlyn was losing $5,000 a year, getting $2,000 back in tax, but still losing $3,000 a year. If she overpaid for a property in a low growth area, then she's made nothing at all out of owning that property.

In general, the higher our income, the higher our tax rate and the higher the negative gearing benefit. Negative gearing is therefore highest for those in Australia earning more than $180,000 a year, because that income is taxed at 47% at time of writing. Even then, making a $5,000 loss and getting $2,350 back in tax is still a $2,650 loss. The capital gain had better outweigh that loss and the buy-in and sell-out costs.

Negative gearing only makes sense where we're buying a property at or below market value, in an area with very good long-term capital growth prospects and when we can hold that property for long enough to make a capital gain – typically seven years plus. If that's not the case, then we're better off using a cash flow strategy and making sure that we cover all the costs with rent.

Once we've got our strategy sorted out, we need to find out what we can afford.

SIX

How Much Can I Borrow?

The three variables banks assess

One of the most commonly asked questions is 'How much can I borrow?', also known as borrowing capacity. Let's look at this in two ways: mathematically and objectively.

Mathematically, how much we can borrow is usually dependent on only three variables:

- Savings or capital
- Income
- Expenses

To buy a property, we have to put down a deposit and pay the costs. If we don't have enough money to cover the deposits and the costs, banks and lenders won't bother looking at our income. They have to protect their interests by always lending less than the value of the property, in case we default on the loan and they have to sell the property.

For savings or capital, the first thing we include is savings in the bank. Savings from overseas can also be counted. Next, we look at potential gifts from family, normally evidenced by a letter. Lastly, we look at equity in another property. If this is a second or third property, maybe we can borrow against the equity in another property to use towards the total. These are used altogether to determine if you've got enough to make the purchase work. Family guarantees will be reviewed in more detail later, but they are a way to use the equity in other family property instead of our own savings.

In Australia, banks prefer to lend at 80% or less of the value of the property, not counting the purchase costs because they can't get those back. Some will still lend up to 95%. As part of a recent election campaign, the government offered to help where a 5% deposit had been saved; hopefully this will be starting in 2020.

To illustrate further, we'll use the examples of two singles, Tom and Sarah. Tom is a technical sales manager with a big phone company earning $180,000/year and has $30,000 in savings. Sarah is a designer for a fashion label earning $100,000, but she has $100,000 in savings.

They would each like to buy a $600,000 property. Tom thinks his $30,000 is 5%, but unfortunately, a $600,000 property attracts $23,000 in stamp duty and there is around $5,000 in legal and other fees to pay. This means Tom would need to get a first home owner's concession on stamp duty and still save another $5,000 before he can buy. Otherwise, he will need to buy a cheaper property for around $500,000. Sarah can cover the purchase costs comfortably and still put down more than 10% as a deposit.

Once the deposit is evidenced, we can look at income after tax, minus any other expenses on a payslip. For a company, we use net profit before tax, plus any wages included in costs, plus any non-cash deductions like depreciation or one-off expenses. Coming back to Tom and Sarah, Tom clearly has the upper hand. Ordinarily $180,000 gross per year would be around $10,400/month after tax, but Tom still has HECS/HELP debt (student loans) and a novated lease for his car. This takes his net pay down to $8,200/month, but it is still more than Sarah's $6,400/month. Without knowing their expenses, we can't yet work out borrowing capacity.

Living expenses are one of the most important weaknesses identified in the 2018 banking Royal

Commission. Most people tend to spend more if they earn more. Banks were typically using a measure of minimum expenditure defined for each household size, regardless of income and other commitments. For a single person, this figure is around $1,500/month, which would leave Tom with $6,700/month and Sarah with $4,900/month left to put towards a mortgage. Their borrowing capacity on this basis would be just under $1m for Tom and just over $700,000 for Sarah.

This weakness has been turned around now by the banks, although it's something we've been doing as brokers for over eight years already. We have to understand how much each household spends, according to what they claim they spend and also what's going through their bank statements.

First, we look at bills. Not just phone, gas, electric, rates and water, but also things like childcare, school fees, gym memberships and insurances. Then we have to add in discretionary spending on things like clothes, holidays and entertainment. We know from basic economics and monetary policy that when interest rates are high people have less money available and spend less, and when interest rates are low they spend more.

Yet, we're currently in an odd situation where banks are looking at what people are currently spending while interest rates are low at around 3.5%, or

HOW MUCH CAN I BORROW?

living at home, but calculating what they can borrow should mortgage rates increase by 2.5% or around 6%. They're almost looking at the worst of both worlds, where spending is at a maximum and the interest rate is at a maximum, despite the probability that the combination will almost never occur.

Back to Tom and Sarah. Sarah lives at home with family and has very few expenses and a credit card limit of $5,000. This is assumed to add $150/month to her expenses. She can comfortably manage on less than $1,500/month, so the bank will use their minimum plus the $150 for the credit card to assume she has $4,750/month for a mortgage as per the table below. She could potentially borrow just under $700,000. With her $100,000 savings, she could actually stretch to buying a property for around $770,000.

	Tom	Sarah
Gross/Year	180,000	100,000
Normal Net/Month	10,400	6,400
HECS/HELP	1,200	0
Novated Lease	800	0
Payslip Net/Month	8,400	6,400
Other Liabilities	500	
Credit Card	600	150
Living Costs	4,000	1,500
Total Costs	6,800	1,650
Net available	3,300	4,750

Tom is renting for $500/week, which will disappear after he buys a place, so we won't count that, but his costs are much higher. He has a personal loan for $22,000 from his last overseas holiday, with repayments of $500/month, and two credit cards, with combined limits of $20,000. This adds $600 to his expense allowance, regardless of how well he manages his cards. His bills and other living expenses come to around $4,000/month. In the table we see he is left with around $3,300 to put towards a mortgage, giving him a maximum loan amount of around $550,000. The $600,000 property is out of Tom's reach for now, but if he implements the five-2 system of bank accounts to control his expenses and build his savings, we can relook at his situation in three to six months' time.

Obviously, it's best to see a qualified broker to get an accurate figure for borrowing capacity, but you can see how important it is to build up savings and control expenses. The example of Sarah and Tom shows the basic maths behind borrowing amounts, and it does give quite wildly different results for different people in different income levels, but that's the reason why we've come up with some rules of thumb.

Rules of thumb to simplify the maths

Never mind what the maths says; how much should we borrow? If expenses are low and income is high and we've got savings or equity or can leverage against a parent's property, then we can buy a very expensive property. In a lot of cases it's not right to buy the most expensive place we can afford, because circumstances can change over time. People assume that property prices go up, but the reality is they don't always do that. The more expensive the property we buy, the more risk we're exposed to in terms of both property price falls and interest rates increasing. For a place to live in, generally speaking, I prefer to keep purchase price to no more than five times annual net income, or four times gross income. For Sarah, earning $100,000 a year, she might be better off buying for $400,000. If interest rates stayed at around 4%, and she contributed 50% of her net income, or 3,200/month, she would clear the loan in under 10 years. The remaining 50% of her income – $3,200 – is much higher than her current $1,500 spending, but it would give her enough to cover the extra costs of living out of home and saving for a holiday each year. In other countries and in Australia in the seventies, 'three times income' was used as a guide.

The second rule of thumb is savings. For Tom, while paying rent he should be able to save around 20% of his income, or $1,640/month. At this rate, it should take him 18 months to reach $30,000 and he should have the deposit for a $1m property in around four years. One of the ways to accelerate savings is to move back in with family and live rent free. If he chooses to do this, it should be possible for him to save at least 50% of income, because we normally spend around

30% on rent. This is one of the reasons Sarah's savings are so high.

The next rule of thumb is to be able to pay off the property in 7 to 10 years. While interest rates are quite low, by putting half your net income towards a home mortgage, it's possible to own a property worth five times your net income, mortgage free in under 10 years. Then it doesn't really matter what happens with interest rates or with market movements. Most mortgages are taken over 30 years, which is how long it takes if you only pay the minimum amount each month. By paying more than the minimum, we can build up a savings buffer and reduce the interest costs. For people on a career path, like Tom and Sarah, their income is at the lowest it's ever going to be, so they might look a little higher. The trick is to accelerate our savings or loan repayments, instead of sticking to the minimum repayment and squandering the rest.

How could/should parents help?

As parents, it's normal to want to help our kids, and as grown-up kids, its normal to want to stand on our own two feet. As long as everyone makes an informed choice as to which way to go, it doesn't matter. My job is to make sure everyone understands the short- and long-term consequences of the three main options before jumping to one based on what a non-professional recommended. The three options for parents wanting to help their children are: gifts, loans and guarantees.

The main reasons to get help from parents are to get into the market more quickly and to eliminate lenders mortgage insurance (LMI). On a $600,000 purchase with a 95% loan, the LMI can be as high as $26,000 – definitely worth eliminating if possible. This cost is what the government may cover in 2020.

Gifts

Gifts are the easiest option for parents with access to funds, but they potentially have the worst long-term outcome. Gary and Julie wanted to help their daughter, Elise, buy her first home and gave her $100,000 towards the purchase. They wanted to lend it to her in case they needed it later, but her bank said it had to be a gift. Elise bought an apartment, using her own savings plus the gift, to have an 80% loan. Elise met John, who moved in shortly afterwards and they quickly merged finances. Four years later, they started to argue about money. John wanted to sell the property and put the equity into a bigger home, but Elise wanted to keep it as a long-term investment. In the end, the arguments over money drove them apart and John insisted the property be sold to get out the equity he had helped to build. Although he wasn't an owner, he'd paid the mortgage down, contributed to repairs and renovated, and it had been his home for four years. The property was sold and the equity divided equally, just to keep the peace. Elise got only half of her original savings and gift back from the sale, and the increase in equity barely covered the other half. After four years, she was no better off than if she'd never bought at all.

Loans

Loans are the preferred option when parents have the funds available or can draw them from their own loan and on-lend them. Had Elise borrowed $100,000 from her parents to buy the property, then they would have been repaid when the property was sold. The equity shared with John would have been $100,000 less, and Elise would have got back her half of the equity, plus been able to re-borrow the $100,000 from her parents for another purchase.

For her next purchase, she repaid the original gift from the equity and then got a loan agreement drawn up by a solicitor to use the $100,000 again. This time around, the bank again tried to say that if it was a loan, they would need to count repayments towards it, which meant she couldn't get the bank loan she needed. However, her broker argued with the bank and got a letter from her solicitor to say that it was a loan with no repayments necessary until, or unless, the property was sold. This was accepted by the bank and the loan was approved.

Guarantees

The third option, for parents who don't have access to spare cash to lend, is a guarantee. This is the option with so much misinformation that it's worth breaking it down further to understand where some of the concerns come from. There are actually two main types of guarantee, with three subtypes, all with different risks and consequences.

Servicing guarantees. This is where someone agrees to make the repayments if the borrower can't. The risk with this type of guarantee is so great that banks now refuse to accept servicing guarantees from anyone other than a spouse.

Security guarantees. There are three subtypes, which we will cover below, but broadly speaking this is where the guarantor offers an additional property to the bank as security. No repayments are required by the guarantors, and the guarantee is only invoked if the loan goes into arrears, the purchased property is repossessed *and* the sale proceeds are not enough to cover the loan. The risks of this depend on the subtype.

The three subtypes are: unlimited, limited and dual loan.

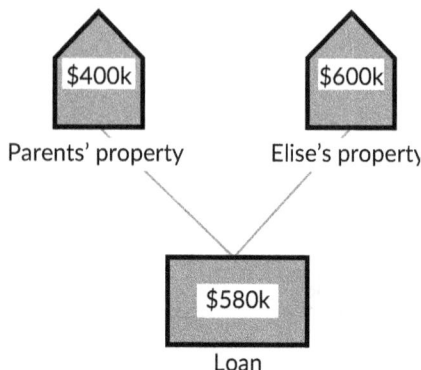

Fig. 6.1

Unlimited' is the easiest subtype to understand. Elise's parents, Gary and Julie, own their own home and an investment property worth around $400,000. Elise could have bought her $600,000 property and the bank would have used that, plus Gary and Julie's $400,000 property, as security. With $600,000 + $400,000 = $1m in property available, the bank would be happy to lend $580,000, which is what she needed. The loan would work out to 580,000/1m = 58%, well below the bank's 80% maximum, and it would be in Elise's name, with Gary and Julie as security guarantors.

What a security guarantee means is that if Elise defaults on her mortgage – not just misses a payment, but defaults – the bank has the right to sell her property and get their money back. And, in this case, if they don't get enough from her property, they have the right to sell the guarantor property too.

Let's imagine a nightmare scenario. The economy is in freefall, Elise gets laid off and can't find another job. She tries moving back home to save on costs, but the tenant she puts into the property also loses their job and stops paying rent. The first time Elise misses a loan payment, she gets a letter from the bank. Same again on the 2nd missed payment. The 3rd missed payment is now serious. Banks in Australia report 90-day arrears to shareholders, and at this point the loan moves over into their legal department. The first thing they do is increase the interest rate by 2%–4%, to help them recover their additional costs. The legal letters get a bit more serious, but it typically takes six to 12 months to repossess a property. The bank tries to sell the property for $600,000, but due to the economic downturn, property prices have dropped and they only get $400,000 for it. They need to recover the remaining $180,000 ($580,000 -$400,000), so they also sell Gary and Julie's investment property.

With an unlimited guarantee, Gary and Julie have no idea how much they might be up for, as they don't know how far property prices might fall. In this example, they'd be up for $180,000, but it could be a lot more, or it might be nothing at all. It's a huge risk and not one any parent should take for their kids.

Limited guarantees put a cap on how much the parents might be up for. In this example, if Elise borrows $580,000, the bank would ask for $725,000 in security. This is because 80% of $725,000 is $580,000, which meets the bank's criteria. If Elise's property is worth $600,000, then Gary and Julie must guarantee up to a maximum of $125,000 ($725,000 - $600,000 = $125,000). Coming back to the nightmare scenario, the bank might be out of pocket by $180,000, but they can only chase Gary and Julie for $125,000. Gary and Julie might choose to repay this to the bank from their savings, rather than lose their investment property. The downside to this option is that even if Elise paid $125,000 off her loan, reducing it to $455,000 ($580,000 - $125,000 = 455,000), the bank might not release the security guarantee. Before releasing the guarantee, they would revalue her property. If its value had fallen to $550,000, they would say her maximum loan is 80% of $550,000 = $440,000. She would need to pay another $15,000 off the loan to release her parents. Gary and Julie might be still be happy with this reduction in their risk, and many banks sign up guarantors this way, but there is a better option.

Dual loans break the problem down into two parts, as shown in Figure 6.2.

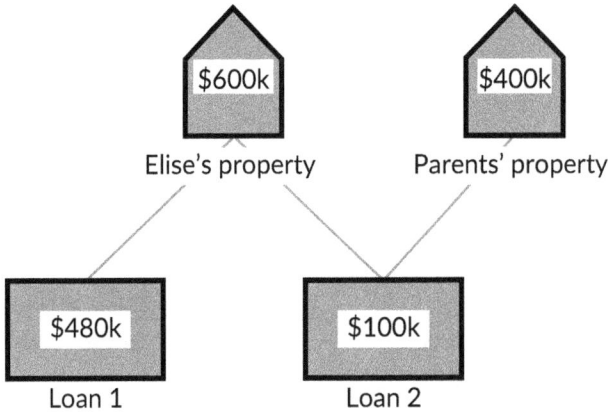

Fig. 6.2

Elise would take out one loan in her name, using her property as security. If she bought for $600,000, the bank would lend 80%, which is $480,000. This loan has nothing to do with Gary and Julie. Elise would then take out a second loan for $100,000, secured by both her property and Gary and Julie's investment property. Their risk has now been cut down to $100,000, which they may have in savings anyway, should the nightmare scenario happen. The other great feature with this structure is that as soon as the $100,000 loan is paid off, Gary and Julie are released, *regardless* of the value of Elise's property. We normally recommend this option, which only a few banks offer, and then suggest that the main 80% loan is repaid over the normal 30-year time period but that the smaller guarantor loan is repaid in five to 10 years. Elise would be confident of being independent from her parents in a shorter timeframe, and Gary and Julie would be happy with the reduced risk.

In this scenario, I deliberately set it up with Gary and Julie's investment property as security, because this option has a much lower risk than using their own home. Some banks will allow parents' homes to be used as security, but the risks have to be considered much more carefully.

I much prefer dual loan security guarantees over paying mortgage insurance, or giving gifts, as there is also a long-term benefit. If the first property could be an investment property in the future, then at that time, the loans used to buy the property would be tax deductible against the rental income (or negative geared). The bigger the loan taken out at purchase, the bigger the future tax deductions and the more cash savings would be available for the future family home. In Elise's case, she could have borrowed $600,000 instead of $580,000 if Gary and Julie were willing to sign up to $120,000 as a guarantee amount. Elise could then have kept hold of $20,000 of her savings, which could be placed in an offset account. This could have kick-started her savings for a future family home.

How much will my repayments be?

Assuming a 10% deposit and using NSW stamp duty figures and first home buyer (FHB) concessions, the table below outlines the deposit amounts and repayments. Repayments are shown as weekly to make it easier to compare them to rent. We've shown the interest cost, because that's the true cost – everything above that is reducing the principal. Also shown are the bank assessed repayments, assuming interest rates jump to 6%. This is what we need to afford to get loan approval, even though the actual cost will be significantly lower at current rates. Until 2016, banks typically used an assessment rate of around 1.5%–2% above current rates; but following pressure from APRA (the Australian Prudential Regulation Authority), banks increased the minimum assessment rate to around 7.25%. In July 2019, APRA have changed to allowing the banks to add 2.5% to the repayment rate. This means on a 3.5% interest rate you would need to be able to afford repayments at 6% instead of 7.25%. Banks have been rolling this out since the APRA changes.

Purchase Price	10% deposit plus costs (NSW)		Weekly interest cost (3.5%)	Weekly P&I cost (3.5%)	Bank assessed P&I cost (6%)
	FHB	Not FHB			
400,000	45,000	58,000	$250	$385	$510
500,000	54,000	73,000	$310	$480	$640
600,000	65,000	87,000	$375	$575	$765
700,000	85,000	102,000	$435	$670	$895
800,000	116,000	116,000	$500	$770	$1,025

What if interest rates rise?

We often get this question, especially from anyone who is risk-averse, but also from anyone who's been around long enough to remember the interest rates of 17% back in 1989/1990 in Australia. Interest rates can change over time and in Australia we can fix for around three or five years. There are a couple of banks that will let you fix for seven to ten years, but the interest rates are so much higher than variable that most won't bother. In other countries, it's completely different; in America you can fix for thirty years and they think that's normal.

The impact of any increase depends on how much you've borrowed relative to your income. As a rough rule of thumb, on a loan of $500,000, a 2% increase in interest rates costs $10,000 per year. Depending on income, $10,000 a year might sound terrifying or quite manageable. Tom (from Chapter Six) on $180,000 a year might not mind a $10,000 swing, but Sarah on $100,000 might opt to fix part of the loan to reduce the risk. On the other hand, if Tom had a property to live in and then bought an investment property, to have loans of $1m, then he might want to fix one of the loans to reduce the $20,000 risk of rates rising by 2%. In general, fixed interest rates are slightly higher than variable. We treat fixed rates a bit like an insurance premium. It's insurance against the risk of interest rates rising.

How long should we take to pay off a loan?

There's a bit of a paradox here, because on the one hand we want debt to go away as fast as possible, but on the other hand we need flexibility to reduce our repayments if circumstances change. It might be possible to repay a loan in 10 years, but if we took a 10-year loan term, and then interest rates shot up, or our circumstances changed, we'd have to try and renegotiate the loan over a longer time frame. We try and take the loan for as long as the bank will allow, such as 30 years, and make additional repayments into either the loan or an offset account while we have the funds to do so. The more we put in our offset account, or pay off our loan, the less interest we pay. If we calculate the 10-year repayment amount and put that into the offset, then use the offset account to make the minimum repayments on a 30-year loan, the offset will build very quickly.

The second question is whether we go for interest only or principal interest. I have the benefit of having property in multiple countries and knowing that the lending rules are different in each country. In the UK, for example, they offer 25-year mortgages on which you only pay interest. After 25 years, the loan has to be refinanced, or paid out in full on the last day. You can't get those in Australia. Most loans described as 'interest only' are principal and interest loans taken over 30 years, but with only interest payable for the first five years. The principal is paid off in the remaining 25 years. For investment properties, some lenders will allow an interest-only period of up to 15 years. This can be quite beneficial for investors, who want to focus all their spare cash on paying off their family home.

In the good old days before 2017, the interest rate was exactly the same whether we went interest only or principal interest, investment or owner-occupied. Now banks have got four different interest rates, with 'owner-occupied principal interest loan' as the cheapest and 'investment interest-only loan' as the most expensive. Part of this difference can be explained by the different capital holding requirements set by APRA. Anything bigger than a 0.1% difference from highest to lowest is just banks taking advantage of differential pricing. The big banks have cranked that all the way up to 1%, a healthy extra 0.9% margin. Deciding whether it's better to pay principal and interest or interest only will depend on the size of the interest rate premium versus the added flexibility from taking interest only.

Imagine Sarah, earning $100,000/year, or $6,400 after tax each month, buys a cute little one-bedroom apartment that she knows is going to be a long-term investment but will live in for a while. When she buys a long-term home for herself, the one-bedroom apartment will be an investment property. If she buys for

$500,000 and has a $100,000 deposit, she has a $400,000 mortgage. Assuming living expenses rise to $3,200 when she moves out of home, she still has $3,200 left.

If Sarah pays principal and interest at $1,900/month on her mortgage but can put $3,200/month in her offset account, then, as the offset account builds, the interest cost will drop. At the start, the interest cost is around $1,320/month, so her $1,900 repayment will take $580 off the principal. With a further $1,300/month off the principal (3,200 - 1,900 = $1,300), she could build her offset account up to $90,000 in five years. At that stage, the bank will charge Sarah interest on $280,000, or around $925/month. They will still insist on principal and interest repayments as if she's paying off the $400,000 (ie at $1,900/month), so every month she is actually reducing the principal by around $975/month. A better option may be to pay just the interest costs on the loan but still put the same $3,200/month into the offset. Although the principal would remain at $400,000, her offset savings in the same amount of time would be around $120,000, instead of $90,000. If she paid interest only, then the $400,000 loan would be tax deductible against any rent and she'd have $120,000 available as a deposit for her family home.

Anything she's paid off that original $400,000 loan can never have interest claimed as tax deductible when the property becomes an investment. If Sarah had paid $3,200/month off the loan, reduced the balance to $280,000 and then redrawn the $120,000 to buy the next property, the bank would see that as one $400,000 loan. Unfortunately, the tax office in Australia will treat her $120,000 redraw as a new loan for the purposes of buying the owner-occupied property. That's why the offset account exists. A good broker can see whether it's worthwhile to pay interest only and pay a slight premium in rate versus paying principal interest and getting the lower rate. It will depend on the long-term position regarding tax deductions. We're not accountants, but there's an equation that we can use to help with the calculations. Of course, check everything with your accountant anyway.

Stage Two: Plan summary

As we've seen, a good plan can make a huge difference. Remember David and Ellie skipping through the five life stages in two steps, without selling, versus Andrew and Zoe buying and selling at every stage?

Part of the right strategy is knowing whether to buy a home, or investment, with an investment decision having its own options. I prefer a combination of investing for cash flow in good capital growth areas together with a home purchase strategy.

Finally, our borrowing capacity will impact what we can and should do. If we can buy a property that can be paid off in seven to 10 years, we will move ahead in leaps and bounds. Getting our preparation right, with the five-2 money diet, will help with both our borrowing capacity and our ability to pay off a home.

With the right preparation completed and a great long-term plan, perhaps we're finally ready to purchase?

PURCHASE

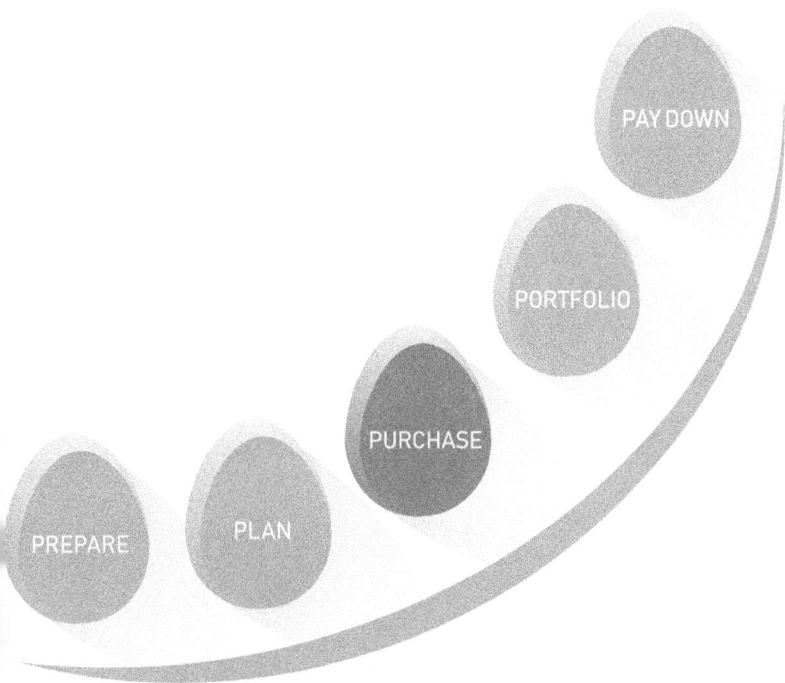

SEVEN

See a Broker

Obviously, I'm biased because I spent 10 years as a broker, which is why I'd always suggest seeing one. In this chapter, I'll explain the difference between a bank and a broker and the difference between a transactional broker and an added value broker.

First, it's important to understand the emotional side of buying a property, because a lot of people don't realise that when you buy your first property it's really scary and exciting. I have a vivid memory of when my clients Todd and Lauren bid at their first auction and they were outbid by $5,000 on a property worth $1.2 million. Lauren was almost throwing up in the gutter after the auction. Needless to say, the next time they went to bid, Todd went on his own and Lauren stayed at home. That's an extreme example, but it is an incredibly emotional time, and until you experience it for yourself you don't know how you're going to react to it.

A bank versus a broker

The big difference between a bank and a broker, apart from the technical side of things, is the emotional side. A broker will typically be the person who you can call on a Saturday, who you can send a text message to and ask if it's okay to bid a little bit more. They are the one that you can call up and ask, 'How does this work, and how does that work, and the agent's saying this and that' and ask what it all means.

For me, the emotional side of things was one of the most enjoyable parts of being a broker. Being with people on that journey to buy property, to be in the thrill of the chase and get the offer just right, and playing with the tactics. The joy when an offer is accepted and knowing that your clients are buying a place is tremendous. Comforting someone after a failed attempt and reassuring them that it'll work out for the best in the long run can make them feel good. If you want someone that's there as a friendly voice to help you along the way, then choosing a broker that you get along with is important.

Let's look at the difference between a bank and a broker. We'll use the Commonwealth Bank as an example.

They run their bank on two streams, which they call channels. The direct channel is the branch network, and the third-party channel is through the brokers. Banks are effectively buying and selling money. They get money from savings accounts or from superannuation funds or from money markets and make a return. Suppose the Commonwealth Bank pays 2% interest on that money and then onsell it through a mortgage at, say, 4%. Their gross profit is 2%. Keep in mind that Australia has four of the ten most profitable banks in the world. From their 2% gross profit, they have to deduct costs associated with their branches or with a broker. In the branch channel, they have to pay the branch rent, heating, lighting, staff salaries and all the paperwork that goes through at the branch level. In the broker channel, they just pay the broker a commission, and then the brokers have to pay for their own rent and heating and lighting and staff and everything else. If you went through a broker who kept you at the same bank you're already with, the broker gets paid a commission. From the bank's perspective, you have the same contract, the same interest rates, the same fees and charges no matter which channel you come through. The only difference is a cost bucket. Either the branch is a cost bucket or the broker is a cost bucket, but for the customer there's no difference.

Let's look at the practical differences between the two. If you do all your banking with one bank, it's probably a mistake and you haven't read Chapter Two, which

I suggest you go back and do now. But your bank knows your savings history, your transaction history, and they can see what you're spending your money on and how much you're spending each month. They also know how much you're earning, so it's relatively straightforward to go into your local branch and ask how much you can borrow. They do a few calculations and get an answer very quickly. Often it's just a system-generated answer, and later their credit department will look at all the evidence in more detail and either reconfirm or decline your application. Branch staff often neglect to mention this process, or that 30% of their customers can't be helped due to their bank policies or calculations.

Going through a broker is a different process. They've got to collect information from scratch, like savings history, spending history, evidence of any liabilities and evidence of your income. They've also got to do identify checks on behalf of whichever bank they recommend, sighting original ID. This is likely to take longer than dealing directly with a bank. In addition, there are further differences, depending on whether you get a transactional broker or an added value broker.

Transactional brokers typically promote themselves based on what they can save you, or the wider choice they can offer, versus just a single bank. They take their customers' circumstances and wants into account and compare the offers of different lenders to find the best deal, including some unadvertised deals which they get from their preferred lenders. Although they may have 20–40 lenders available, most brokers put all their business through three to five lenders because it's much easier for them to understand the policies and processes of those three to five lenders.

Added value brokers will use their experience to question and challenge why their customers are buying a property of a particular type or value. They'd ask whether the client would be better off long term by borrowing less or waiting until they are better prepared. They will recommend the right loan structure to suit long-term needs and educate their clients on things like fixed or variable, principal and interest versus interest only, and using guarantors versus paying LMI. They'll typically work with a wider array of lenders because they are looking for the best outcome for customers rather than the easiest transaction for themselves.

In my company, I found that over 60% of the decisions we made on lender choice came down to lender policy, rather than interest rate. Different lenders have different policies around bonuses, or commission income, or probation periods, or contract income. There are wide differences in the types of property banks will lend against and the way guarantors are handled. Most banks align themselves with one of two mortgage insurance companies (QBE or Genworth), and there can be big differences in the premiums or policies of each of the two insurers. Some lenders allow multiple offset accounts, which can be good for the different types of savings accounts. The best lender is usually the one that gives you what you want at a cost that you're prepared to pay.

In simple terms, it's difficult to work out from a Google search whether what you want to do makes sense and which lenders will be happy to lend to you, or if the interest rate is the most important element. A good broker who you connect with on a personal level will help get the right outcome for your circumstances and long-term needs and help to calm you down when things are tense.

Are pre-approvals worth it?

'Pre-approval' is a generic industry term, but there are others, like 'conditionally eligible' or 'conditional approval', that mean the same thing. It normally means that the lender has assessed the customer's ability to borrow an amount of money, up to a percentage of the property value. For example, a pre-approval for $400,000 or up to 80% of the purchase property means they will either lend 80% of $500,000 or, if the purchase price was only $450,000, then they will lend 80% of $450,000, which is $360,000.

Legally, you don't need a pre-approval. They do help us feel comfortable and more confident in our ability to borrow money, though. Some people, with a good amount of savings and great incomes, in stable jobs, who want to borrow a relatively modest amount compared to their incomes can probably get a loan anywhere. They don't need a pre-approval at all, and each application will be listed on their credit file and reduce their credit score. For other people – for example, those borrowing over 80% of the value of the property, maybe with overtime or bonus income or who've not been in the job very long – a pre-approval is definitely recommended.

Unfortunately, a pre-approval is no guarantee of finance. Some of them are only approved electronically, and a pre-approval is automatically generated by the lender. It may be the case that none of the paperwork has been verified by the lender's credit team. Even a credit-assessed pre-approval can fall over at the next stage. To get an unconditional approval or formal approval, the credit team have to agree to lend money for you to buy the particular property at the price you paid.

We had one case recently where a client was pre-approved and went and bid successfully at auction. The bank valuer went out to look at the property and the bank said that for properties in that area they would only lend 70% of the value of the property, not 80%. Suddenly they were going to charge mortgage insurance to lend 80%, which was going to make it really expensive. Fortunately, we were able to get an approval with another lender, one who hadn't changed their policies on properties in that area.

To get pre-approved, the first question is, 'How much can we borrow?' For the pre-approval, we always need to ask for more than is needed. When a client says they want to buy a place for $500,000, a good broker will always ask, 'What if the perfect place was $510,000?' In that situation, they would normally set an absolute maximum, of say $550,000. The final loan will be a percentage of the purchase price of the property. Pre-approval might be for 90% of $550,000 = $495,000, but the target might be around $500,000 and the final purchase could be as low as $450,000. The final loan amount would be 90% of $450,000 = $405,000.

The second key question with pre-approvals is, 'How long do they last?' The average in the industry is about three months, after which they lapse. Renewing often requires another round of payslips, savings statements and bank forms, and each one will be recorded on the individual's or couple's credit files. Too many pre-approvals or renewals could make the file look bad. Some lenders claim their pre-approval lasts for six or twelve months but will still ask for pay slips and bank statements if the pre-approval is older than three months at the time of purchase. One or two lenders only offer 30-day pre-approval.

The last consideration for the pre-approval is the lender restrictions – specifically, on things like size of property for smaller units. In Australia, apartments smaller than 50 square metres internally will have restrictions for some lenders. Different lenders have their own benchmarks, and then the two big mortgage insurance companies (QBE and Genworth) have their own benchmarks, too. At the time of writing, Genworth requires a minimum of 40 square metres internally, regardless of balcony and garage, and QBE requires 50 square metres in total, regardless of how much is internal and how much is in the balcony and garage. Before putting in an offer, it's important to check these things and adjust if necessary.

An experienced broker will tell you whether you need a pre-approval or whether it's a nice-to-have. If a bank gives you a pre-approval within an hour, or on the spot, it just means they punched the numbers into their system. It doesn't necessarily mean that the credit department have looked at the paperwork and will agree with the staff member who gave the pre-approval. Either way, it's the unconditional approval that matters, which can only be completed after the contract has been signed, the price agreed and the lender agrees to accept the property as security for the loan.

As I said at the beginning, I'm biased; but a good, value-added broker can be a great asset, especially when buying your first home. Signing a contract for half a million dollars or more is pretty scary, so make sure you know if a lender will back you beforehand and what some of their restrictions might be.

EIGHT

Property Analysis And Tips

In this chapter, I'd like to give some top tips on what to look for in a property and some of the things to be careful of. Properties are typically the most expensive things we will ever buy, and the loans for them are the most debt we will ever get into. We need to make sure that we're not buying a dud. We'll look at some of the statistics for different property markets around Australia. We'll also look at how to do research on specific properties when you find them. For investment properties, it's important to understand depreciation, which may have an impact on taxation costs. It's also important to properly calculate costs and returns, both short- and long-term, for any investment property. And for any property, it's important to understand how fast the loan can be repaid.

Why there's more than one property market

The fastest way to drive me – or anyone else who knows anything about property – up the wall is to ask what the property market is doing. The less irritating option is to ask whether now is a good time to buy (given the current market). To put it plainly: there is no single market for property in Australia.

There's not even one single market for property in New South Wales or Sydney. The 'property' sphere has many small adjacent markets within each city which can move at different rates at different times.

For example, in Sydney there's a difference between buying an apartment in the Inner West or a house in the Inner West, but there are some similarities and some overlap. But there's a huge difference between buying an apartment in the Inner West and a house on the North Shore. They are two different markets that can behave in different ways at different points in time. The same applies when you look at, for example, the eastern suburbs of Sydney, like Bondi and Double Bay. And then you look at the outer suburbs of Sydney, like Campbelltown or Camden. Following the global financial crisis of 2008, most of Sydney continued on a normal growth path as if nothing had happened, except for some high value houses in good suburbs and houses more than 40km from the city. House prices in Brisbane move almost completely independently of Sydney, which is 1,000km away.

It's important to look at any property in its own right relative to its recent history in the area and not be comparing it to other markets which are completely unrelated.

Property research and buyer's agents

As we've said before, it's important to make sure that you're not getting ripped off on such an expensive asset. It's also important to feel comfortable in your ability to research the property or in your ability to negotiate. Otherwise, just hire a buyer's agent.

A buyer's agent is different to a seller's agent because you pay them to do the job for you. They will do the research, they'll tell you which areas to go for, which properties to go for and how much to pay for a property, and they'll negotiate the whole thing for you. They'll typically charge around a couple of percent of the purchase price. In the US market, everyone has a buyer's agent to understand their needs and negotiate for them. US seller's agents tend to just list a property online and then wait for buyer's agents to ring up and negotiate with them.

Of course, there's no substitute for going out and looking at property, and for 10 years I spent my weekends at open homes with real estate agents because there's always people looking for help and it's interesting to meet new people. You realise that each property is unique. Is it close to the train station? Does it have an internal or external laundry? Are the bathrooms recently renovated, or old and dated? Does the living space have enough room to put a TV on one wall and bookshelves on another? Is the balcony big enough to put a barbecue out there? All these things, plus the number of bedrooms/bathrooms/garages, make us want to buy the place or not. At the end of the day, it still comes down to numbers. We want to know if that property is worth the price that they're asking and what we're willing to pay.

One of the best tools for researching property in Australia is from a company called RP Data. Several banks offer their reports online, but a good broker also offers their information free of charge. They provide a very quick report on each property showing a range of values for similar properties in the same area. It's only a range because unless someone physically looks at that property, they can't tell you whether it's one of the best or worst in the area. The report will give you a range and a percentage standard deviation.

Let's say we see a property that we quite like valued at $600,000 by the agent. The property report gives it a figure of $570,000, with a range of $520,000–$620,000. That $100,000 swing represents a deviation of around 10% either side of the midpoint. Our own research, or our buyer's agent's research, will tell us whether the property we've seen should be at the high or low end of the range. When we should worry is when we see a midpoint of $570,000 and a range of $520,000–620,000 and the agent is asking $650,000. Some unscrupulous agents also quote below the range to try and get more buyers to show up at auction. Unfortunately, selling agents are not there to do us buyers any favours as they are working for the seller. Their job is to get as much money out of us as possible and as much money out of the market as possible. There are laws against underquoting in some states, but those laws are not necessarily fully enforced or enforced on a particular property.

I've used a buyer's agent for most of the properties I've bought. This is partly because I often buy outside of the area that I live in, but also to save money. We settled on a property in March this year, which we were happy to buy for the advertised price of $595,000. Our buyer's agent negotiated another $35,000 off the cost of the property – more than triple their fee.

Another source of free research available in Australia is https://realestate.com.au. Most of us are used to just going onto the web page, keying in the suburb and then pulling up properties that meet our brief. Further down the front page is a button labelled 'Research Suburbs'. From there, we can key in the suburb, scroll down or hit 'Price'. The latter initially shows us the buy and rent price for houses, split by number of bedrooms. Two further tabs take us to similar info for units, and then 'Trend' shows a rolling 12-month price history for houses and units. By clicking 'Annual' underneath the graph, we can see nine years' history of prices for that suburb. I'd encourage any investor to look not just at today's value but also the long-term trend in your chosen area.

If we do our property research correctly, or employ an expert if needed, we won't overpay for a property.

Depreciation benefits short and long term

Depreciation laws changed in September 1987, with further changes to depreciation in May 2017. As a result, it's crucial to know whether a property was built before or after the 1987 changes. The 2017 changes relate to newly built properties only.

Depreciation in property seems very strange, since we normally buy property expecting it to appreciate in value. However, a newer property will typically sell for more than an older one in the same area. As the value of land and property in an area rises, the value of the bricks and mortar, or fixtures and fittings, are actually falling. This is the essence of depreciation.

In most businesses, if a business buys a piece of equipment for more than $30,000 that lasts for several years, it can't just write off the cost of that purchase in the first year; the business depreciates it over its useable life. A machine costing $100,000 and expected to last 10 years will be written off at the rate of $10,000/year. This means that each year for 10 years the business will claim a tax deduction of $10,000 for the depreciation of the machine.

Property is a little more complex, but it starts from the same basis. Since the 1987 changes, a building is assumed to have a 40-year life, equivalent to 2.5% per year. That means if it cost $100,000 to build in 1990, the building will be assumed to last until 2030, dropping by $2,500/year in value. When we buy a property to live in, we can't count this value drop. For investment properties, we would deduct that $2,500/year from the rent we receive before paying any taxes. If Caitlyn from Chapter Five was losing $5,000/year based on rent, less interest and costs, and had bought a 1990 property with a $100,000 build cost, then she could add $2,500 to her taxable loss, to bring it to $7,500. She would then get $2,588 back in tax but have only paid out $5,000 in cash losses. The depreciation schedule has helped her to get back over half her losses, or an extra $863, versus making the same loss on a pre-1986 property.

Up until May 2017, every investment property purchase, no matter the age of the building, could claim depreciation on the fixtures and fittings. For example, if we bought a 100-year-old property for $600,000, it was assumed that part of the purchase price was going towards the cooker, air conditioner, wall coverings, floor coverings, water heater, etc. A quantity surveyor could write a report to say that those items were worth, say, $15,000, and this might be written off over a period of, say, five years. This would have added $3,000/year to the depreciation schedule. If you happened to own an investment property prior to May 2017, you may still be able to back-claim the depreciation for up to four previous tax years.

Since May 2017, only brand-new fixtures and fittings that you buy yourself, or buy direct from the builder as part of a new property purchase, can be depreciated. Even if we buy a property built one year ago, with another five to 10 years' depreciable life left on the fixtures and fittings, we can't claim anything on them.

The total depreciation amount is therefore building plus fixtures and fittings, for brand-new properties, or just building, for properties built from September 1987 onwards.

> The more depreciation you claim, the more capital gains tax you pay when you sell.

Some people, and even some accountants, use this half-fact as a reason not to claim depreciation, but they are missing two key pieces of information. Let's use an example. George and Tatiana bought a 2001-built property that they knew would be an investment. The property cost $1m, but the building could be depreciated at $5,000/year. They sold after six years, by which time their original $1m purchase cost was reduced by $5,000/year. The $5,000 reduction for six years gave them a cost base of $970,000 ($1m–$30,000). At that time, if the property sold for $1.5m, their capital gain is assumed to be $530,000, rather than $500,000 ($1m–$500,000), which is what it would have been if they had never claimed depreciation. But:

1. There is a 50% capital gains tax (CGT) concession available, which reduces George and Tatiana's taxable gain to $265,000, only $15,000 higher than it would have been on $500,000 profit (50% of $500,000 = $250,000). This means they claimed $30,000 in deductions over six years and now only get taxed on $15,000 extra as a result.

2. The reason George and Tatiana sold after six years is because they were taking career breaks in order to travel. Their tax rate while they were claiming the depreciation was 39%, whereas they will only pay around 30% tax on the capital gains because they sold in a low-income year.

I always aim to keep property until retirement, which means if I choose to sell any of my properties any capital gains I make will be taxed at a lower rate than during my working life. Depreciation shouldn't be the only reason to buy a property, but it does impact the tax costs of owning an investment.

How much will my investment property cost per year?

For an investment property, we need to do our calculations properly to know what our expenses will be month to month and year to year. A good investment calculator will allow us to quickly compare one property with another to see how each will work out. We don't want to just buy a property for $600,000 and hope it's going to double in 10 or 15 years, without comparing it to other ones that might double over the same timeframe but cost less each year to hold. By the way, I'm more conservative than others in terms of property growth and typically assume 14–24 years to double.

The first element for our investment calculations is how much we put down as a deposit, with two opposing schools of thought:

1. The bigger the deposit you put in, the lower the loan amount and the lower the interest costs each year.

2. To grow a portfolio quickly, the less you put in, the faster you can buy the next one. Also, if you invest before you buy a long-term family home, the less you put into your investment, the more you'll have for a family home and the smaller the non-deductible loan you will have.

The second thing that impacts our returns is the interest rate that we're paying on the loan. At the time of writing, there are good three- and five-year fixed rates in Australia. Otherwise, if we select variable rates, then we need to estimate long-term averages rather than necessarily going by what they are today. It's always better to be more conservative with the interest rate that we put into our calculations. Only the interest is deductible, and there's typically a difference in interest rate for interest only versus principal and interest, which we'll cover in a later section.

For people that already own their own home, the priority is to pay that off before paying off any investment properties. This will be covered in more detail in the *Pay Down* section, but in summary: *Always* pay the home loan off before investment properties.

The next set of costs are the other property-related costs, such as strata, maintenance and repairs, council rates, water rates and insurance. Normally we need buildings insurance on a house and strata covers buildings insurance for an apartment, but we always recommend taking landlord's insurance for an investment property. This protects you against malicious damage by the tenant, legal costs associated with rent recovery, and lost rent in the event of a fire or similar building problem that renders the property uninhabitable. Be aware that it doesn't cover rental vacancies between tenancies, though.

The next cost is the managing agent. This is important even if we buy a property near where we live.
Otherwise, we are giving ourselves an extra job to do
for which we may not be qualified. We'd also be taking
on all of the risks of choosing the right tenant, vetting
them, collecting rent, hassling the tenant when they
don't pay on time, figuring out what a fair market rent
is and putting rents up every six to 12 months. I've got
multiple properties, in many locations, so I couldn't
possibly manage all of them. Do shop around for an
agent, and not just on the basis of fees. Understand
their inspection processes, because some agents are
diligent and will go and visit the property every four or
six months and other agents won't look at the property
from one year to the next. Usually the agent charges
a percentage of the value of the rent; in Sydney that's
around 5% or 6% and in Brisbane it's typically around
7% or 8%, but it does vary by city or by area.

The last cost to take into account with your property
is vacancies. A low vacancy rate is around 2% or 3%,
which doesn't sound like a lot, but 2% is equivalent
to one week's rent per year. Vacancies typically add
to agent fees for re-letting and advertising, which can
cost another week's rent.

Rent minus all of the expenses will give us a loss, a
profit or breaking even. If a property is making a loss,
then in Australia we say it's negatively geared. The
loss gets bigger, or the profit is reduced, based on the
depreciation schedule, to determine the tax payable,

or refund. Depreciation is removed again to figure out the net cost to own or profit from owning the investment.

With rent, we mustn't take the selling agent's word for it. They are trying to sell us the property – probably because they've run out of grandmas to sell. They might think it will rent for $500 to $550 a week but only tell us $550. We should get an independent assessment and use the lower figure in the range. Your broker should be able to run an RP Data rental valuation for you.

PRO-TIP

If someone is offering a rental guarantee, ignore it and get suspicious.

One of the cheapest tricks for a selling agent is to pretend a property's worth a lot more than it is and give you a rental guarantee that matches their quote. For example, if an agent was selling a property worth $500,000 and it would rent for $450 a week, they could quote a $600,000 valuation, with a $550-a-week rental guarantee. Rental guarantees normally only last one to two years and the agent or developer only pays the shortfall. In this example, it will cost them $100 a week, or $5,200 for a one-year guarantee, and only $10,400 for a two-year guarantee. Paying $10,000 to get a $100,000 price hike is a great investment for them, not so good for us. I always get a different local agent to give me a rental appraisal and never use the selling agent.

How much faster can I pay it off?

Now, this might seem an odd thing to look at when researching a property, but if we're going to buy a place to live in, then the question of how fast we can pay it off or quickly reduce the amount of interest that we're paying is an important one. As I've said before, a valuable long-term strategy is to own a place with no mortgage. If the property is going to become an investment in the future, we would have an offset account and quickly build that up until it matches the home loan. A $500,000 loan with a $500,000 offset account is charged $0 in interest.

As a rough guide, a first home you can pay off in seven to 10 years will get you ahead over the long-term. Mortgages are normally over 30 years, but we need to ask if it could be paid off over seven to 10 years, using 50% of income for a home, or 20% if it's an investment and we are renting. If we can eliminate the mortgage, then we won't care what happens with house prices. Stretching and struggling to pay a loan off over 25 to 30 years puts us at risk of the market falling, rates rising, or a sudden drop in income, or all of the above. The only reason to consider something which will take longer to pay off is if we're certain of a dramatic upswing in income. For example, if the property is affordable on one income, but when a partner returns to work the loan can be annihilated.

As a rough guide, at around 4% interest rate, doubling the 30-year P&I repayment amount, would cut the term to under 11 years, and 2.5 times the repayment amount cuts it to just over eight years.

If you already have a property, or are revisiting this book following your first purchase, then the next question is, 'What should I do with the first one?'

NINE

Sell Or Keep Your First

Priya and Rahul bought their first property, a two-bedroom apartment in Alexandria, for $400,000, without any clear strategy in mind of where they were going to go long term. It is now worth $600,000 and they want to upgrade to plan for a family.

In this chapter, we're going to look at their decision in detail. We'll start with some of the costs in selling or keeping, then determine whether or not they can release equity from the property if they keep it. Next, we'll figure out how to structure their finances to put them in a good position if they keep it long term. Then we'll look at a clever trick, using a line of credit, which may help them in the longer term. My attitude is always to try and keep the first property, if possible.

Selling costs and consequences

If Priya and Rahul sell their apartment, there are costs to cover. The biggest of those are the selling agent costs, which are typically around 2% of the value of the property, but advertising costs may be even more. Priya and Rahul were pleased to negotiate only a 1.5% fee with the prospective agent, but we pointed out that once the $4,000 advertising was included, they would spend $13,000 if they sell for $600,000, or 2.2% of the value.

PRO-TIP

When I've sold property, I never agree a flat percentage.

I have a really low percent up to the bare minimum price that any muppet could get and then 5%–10% commission for everything above that. Agents try to win business by talking up the price they will get for you, so I use that against them. In Priya and Rahul's case, the agent had said he could get $650,000–700,000 for their property. They could offer 1% up to $600,000, and 8% for everything above $600,000. If the agent achieved their dream price of $700,000, he would be paid $14,000 (1% x $600,000 = $6,000; 8% x $100,000 = $8,000; $6,000 + $8,000 = $14,000). A $14,000 fee is 2% of $700,000, which is the commission the agent wanted at the price he said he could get. But now if he only sells for the normal market price of $600,000, he will only be paid $6,000 instead of the 1.5% figure of $9,000.

The next costs are those associated with paying off the existing mortgage. There are state government fees for releasing the mortgage from the property and bank fees for discharging the mortgage. In addition, if Priya and Rahul had a fixed rate loan then there may be some break costs associated with it. The only way to figure that out is to ring the bank and ask them. Priya and Rahul owe $278,000 on a variable rate mortgage, so they only have around $700 in government and bank fees to pay.

Then there are solicitor/conveyancer fees to sell. These fees are often bundled up with buying costs, but they typically add another $1,000–$2,000 to the costs of selling.

Lastly, CGT could be an issue if the property was an investment for any period of the ownership. Best to check with an accountant to be sure whether this applies to you. In Rahul and Priya's case, they have lived in the property the whole time, so there will be no CGT to pay.

The other concept most people don't take into account is the cost of rebuying a similar property. If they sold and later wanted an equivalent investment property, it will cost them around $27,000 in stamp duty and legal fees to buy it.

To summarise, selling will cost Priya and Rahul around $15,000, with an additional $27,000 opportunity cost if they wanted to buy a similar property as an investment later. If they sell for $600,000, less $15,000 in costs and a $278,000 mortgage, they would have $307,000 towards the next purchase.

Income, long-term plans and risk

As I've said, my bias is always to try and keep the property if we can, but whether we can depends on income and long-term plans. The good news for Priya and Rahul is that rent becomes their third source of income, after their two salaries, which will add $500/week. Unfortunately, when we look at finance, banks only count 80% of rental income, assuming 20% disappears in agent fees, vacancies, insurances, etc. Even if Priya and Rahul take an interest-only investment loan on the Alexandria property, paying only $240/week, most banks will want them to be able to afford P&I repayments at 6% = $390/week. They will be comfortable receiving $500/week and paying $240/week in interest, but the bank will use $400/week as their rental income and $390/week for their repayment, which is only a $10/week surplus.

The other interesting area to think about is spreading the portfolio risk, covered in more detail in Stage Four, *Portfolio*. In this example, Priya wants a home in Ryde, which is north west of the city, versus Alexandria on the south side, in the Inner West. Buying a second property in Ryde would give them a home and an investment property in slightly different areas, which could work long term. If they were buying a home in the same area, it might make sense to offload the Alexandria unit and buy an investment property in a different area in the future.

Equity release without selling

The alternative to selling their first property is to release the equity in the property. For Rahul and Priya, they could increase their loan up to 80% of the current value, which would be $480,000 (80% x $600,000). This will give them $202,000 ($480,000 - $278,000 = $202,000) towards their next purchase without selling. At 88%, they could take an extra $48,000 = $250,000 total.

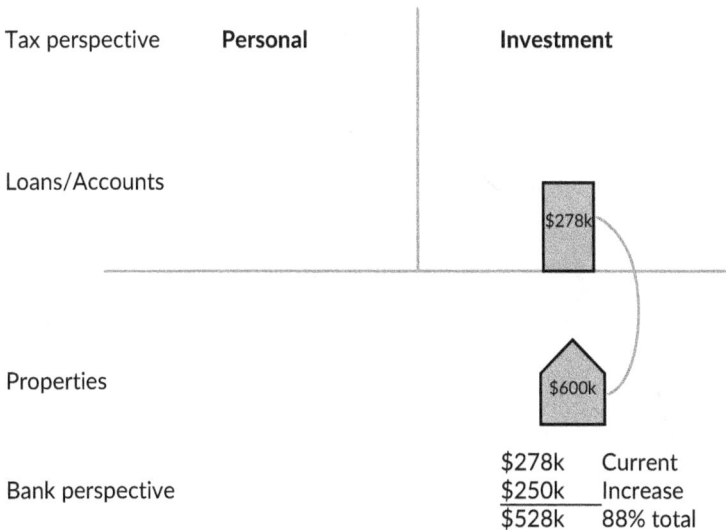

Tax perspective	**Personal**	**Investment**
Loans/Accounts		$278k
Properties		$600k
Bank perspective		$278k Current
		$250k Increase
		$528k 88% total

Fig. 9.1

Their example is typical of many, where releasing equity is more efficient than selling the property, yielding almost as much as selling after deducting the other costs associated with it.

Loan structure for flexibility and easier tax time

There's one right way and two wrong ways to release home equity. Priya and Rahul want to buy a property for $1m in Ryde. Most banks would simply take both properties as security and lend them an extra $1.045m to cover the purchase price plus costs, secured by both properties. That's wrong for two reasons. First, banks like to lend 80%, and the total borrowing of $1.045m + $278,000 = $1.323m is now 83% of the total equity of $1.6m. This means the bank will charge them around $15,000 in LMI. The second problem is that the properties are now linked together, which is often called 'crossing' or 'cross-securing'. This means Priya and Rahul can't sell or refinance either property in the future without impacting the other. A good value-added broker will point out the long-term loss in flexibility and control of doing this.

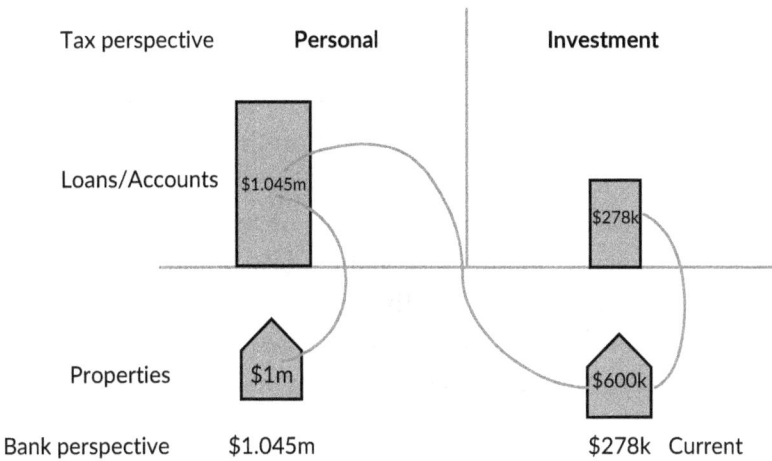

Tax perspective	**Personal**		**Investment**
Loans/Accounts	$1.045m		$278k
Properties	$1m		$600k
Bank perspective	$1.045m		$278k Current

Fig. 9.2

The second wrong way would be to increase the current loan from $278,000 to $528,000 (88% of $600,000). On the one hand, it would lower the LMI bill to around $9,000, while providing enough funds to cover a 20% deposit; but on the other hand, it would make Priya's and Rahul's future tax returns difficult. Although a bank will allow them to increase the loan from $278,000 to $528,000, the ATO will see the $278,000 loan amount as used for the investment property and the $250,000 extra as owner-occupied debt because it was used to buy their home. In Australia, our tax deductibility is based on the purpose the funds were taken for, not the security offered to the bank.

The right way to do it is to get a separate loan for $250,000, secured by the Alexandria property, which we know is non-deductible. Some lenders will charge a lower interest rate on this, and tax time is now much easier. Interest charged on the $278,000 loan will be deductible, and interest charged on the $250,000 and $800,000 loans will be non-deductible. Priya and Rahul could also elect to pay interest only on the $278,000 loan and principal and interest on the $250,000 and $800,000 loans. In the short term, they might take the $250,000 as an interest-only loan until the new purchase settles. The recommended structure is shown in Figure 9.3.

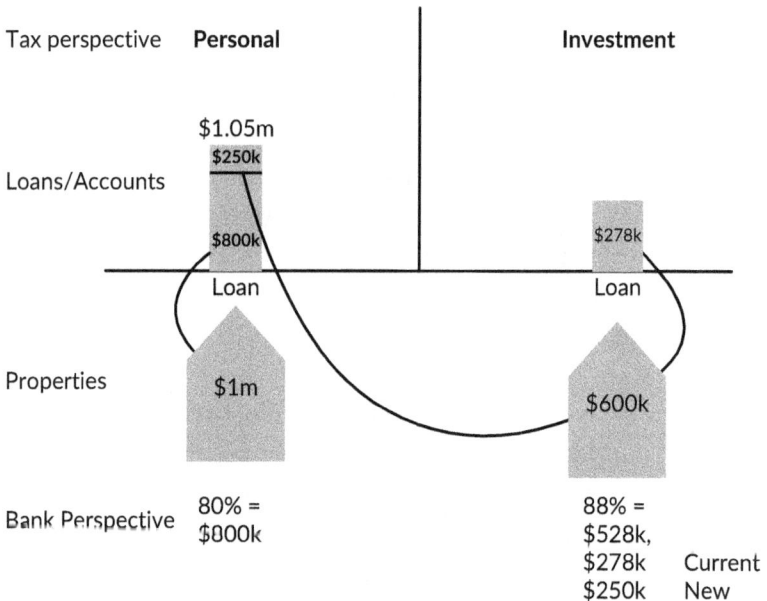

Tax perspective	Personal		Investment
	$1.05m		
	$250k		
Loans/Accounts			$278k
	$800k		
	Loan		Loan
Properties	$1m		$600k
Bank Perspective	80% = $800k		88% = $528k,
			$278k Current
			$250k New

Fig. 9.3

We always recommend taking the additional loan first, even before finding a place to buy. In this example, the $250,000 would be available to redraw, partly for the 10% contract deposit and the remainder for the purchase settlement. The $250,000 loan would be paid into itself to begin with, so Priya and Rahul would have a zero-balance loan with a $250,000 limit. If it's interest only, then there will be nothing to pay until the money is used. It's also easier to get the top-up loan approved first, and this avoids delays in the purchase approval during the finance clause or cooling off period. We don't necessarily have to use the same bank for both loans. We can choose the best one for each purpose.

It's important in these examples to separate out personal and investment, so every transaction, whether for the property purchase or ongoing rent and expenses, can be separated.

How a line of credit reduces risk

A line of credit (LOC) is an unusual bank product because it's like a big overdraft secured by property. LOCs can be quite useful when we've got plenty of equity in our home for a number of reasons. The first is that they give us the flexibility to take money whenever we want. The main difference compared to a loan account is that a LOC is fully transactional. It can be used to pay bills and make other loan repayments, and it can also have a positive balance as well as a negative balance with most lenders. By comparison, a loan only has a negative balance and can't be used to make repayments on another loan.

There are two reasons why I use or recommend a LOC. Firstly, we use it for our investment property repayment account. We make sure that the rent and any transactions to do with the investment property go through the LOC. This allows us to manage the property separately from any personal accounts. When it comes time to do tax returns, we simply pull up the LOC statements and all the transactions are for the investment property.

The second benefit is that if a property is running at a slight loss, or if there's a vacancy, then we're effectively borrowing the money to cover that loss, which should be deductible. Always be sure to check with an accountant.

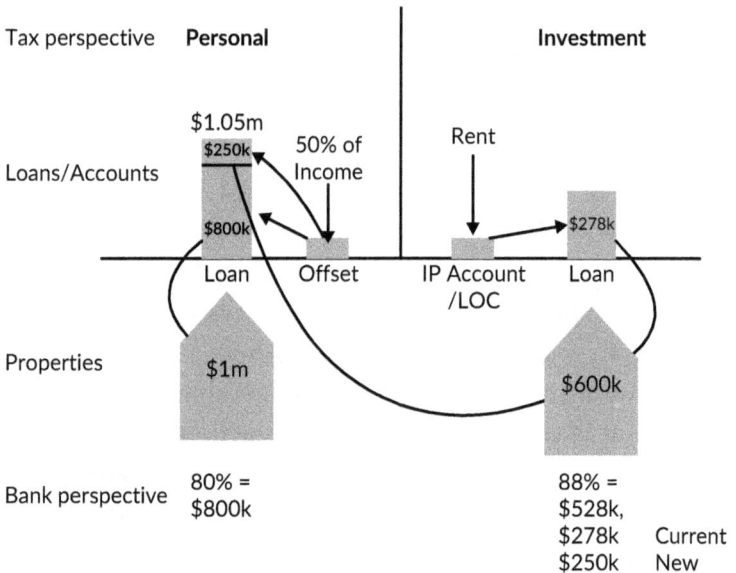

Tax perspective	**Personal**			**Investment**	
	$1.05m				
	$250k	50% of Income	Rent		
Loans/Accounts					$278k
	$800k				
	Loan	Offset	IP Account /LOC	Loan	
Properties	$1m				$600k
Bank perspective	80% = $800k			88% = $528k, $278k Current $250k New	

Fig. 9.4

The other reason we use a LOC is because at the moment in Australia there's a big difference between interest rates for interest-only loans and principal interest loans. A LOC lets us get the lower interest rate for principal and interest repayments, with the LOC covering any gap from the rent. A property is more likely to run at a loss on a cash basis, but instead of taking our own funds to cover the principal, the LOC covers it. This means we can still use all our personal funds to build an offset or pay off a forever home.

Stage Three: Purchase summary

Buying property is risky and scary, and in my biased opinion, it's better to do it with the help of a good, added value broker than on your own. We can reduce the risks by researching properly, using a buyer's agent and buying well within our means.

Once we've bought one property, we need to seek help to structure our loans and bank accounts properly to make it possible to keep additional properties. Three or more properties would be considered a portfolio, which is much more complex and needs its own stage…

PORTFOLIO

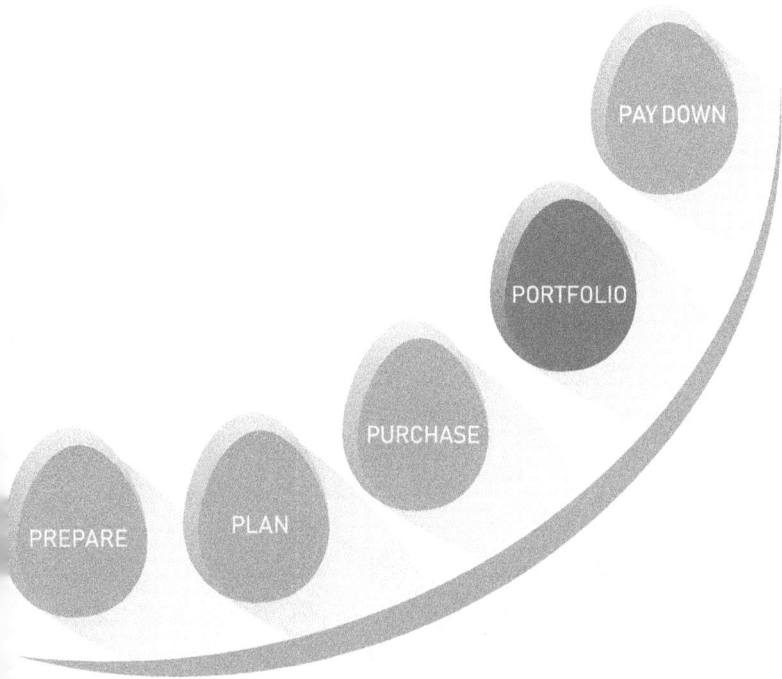

TEN

Why I Love Property

How the numbers stack up

Most financial planners argue against buying investment property, claiming that shares outperform property. The common argument is that long-term share growth is 8% and long-term property growth is 5%, so shares win. This ignores the impact of gearing, or borrowing, which means that if we put $60,000 into a $400,000 property, that 5% growth is on $400,000 = $20,000/year, versus 8% on $60,000, which is only $4,800.

The table below shows a worked example of property versus shares, including inflation. Assumptions: 2% inflation, 4% property price growth, 8.2% share growth. If the property makes a loss, this could be covered by savings, so we've added that amount to the shares each year. If the property makes a profit, it's assumed that this amount is paid off the loan. Net equity after costs includes selling costs, but not CGT, although property gets a concession on that versus shares.

$585,000 property rented at $450/week (4%) yield

	Start	Year 5	Year 10	Year 20
Deposit/shares	91,744	153,684	245,332	558,592
Annual rent	23,400	25,835	28,524	34,771
Annual net loss	-3,355	-3,357	-2,251	319
Net equity after costs	55,645	184,557	341,398	764,739
Property vs shares	-36,099	30,872	96,066	206,148

$585,000 property rented at $550/week (5%) yield

	Start	Year 5	Year 10	Year 20
Shares/deposit	91,744	136,888	203,152	446,780
Annual rent	28,600	31,577	34,863	42,498
Annual net loss	-436	-109	1,396	5,555
Net equity after costs	55,645	185,568	346,252	804,655
Property vs Shares	-36,099	48,680	143,100	357,875

The second table shows that by buying a slightly higher-yielding property, the results favour property more strongly and the annual net loss is removed more quickly.

My properties

In 2008, we started our investing journey. We already had a property in Sydney but were living in the UK. The global financial crisis was just kicking off and I thought it was the right time to start investing. I decided to invest in some cash positive properties in the UK. For me that was important because I've got family in the UK, so will always want to go back and visit. In particular, I needed to offset any changes in the exchange rate, which might make the Australian dollar worth a lot less and travel less affordable.

I bought through a buyer's agent who specialised in buying below-market-value properties, so at a time when the market had just dropped about 10%, they were finding properties a further 10% lower. I bought at what ended up being the bottom of the market because those market segments fell about 20%. We ended up with three terrace houses in the north west and north east of England, in fundamentally good locations within the cities that they're in, but that were long-term cash positive.

We moved back to Australia and started looking at other strategies, initially trying to fund my retirement back into teaching. By 2010, the global financial crisis had bitten hard in some countries and there were some really great opportunities over in America. I researched different areas, based on population size (cities of over one million people) and good long-term population growth, settling on Phoenix. We bought in 2011, and, as luck would have it, 2011 was the very bottom of the market, which had continued to fall for four years after the global financial crisis.

We bought small blocks of apartments, two in good locations and another in a not-very-good location, with vendor finance available. This meant that we only paid a small deposit and the seller lent us the balance. We've since sold that third property because it wasn't a strategic property for us. At the same time, we bought a unit in a retirement community 40km from Brisbane, which looked very cash positive but had huge management costs and very low resale value. That's the only property we've since sold for a loss.

We continued to invest, but this time in Australia and bought a place in Queensland. I believe the Sunshine Coast is a good long-term play. I think it's going to be a big area in the next 20 to 30 years. At the moment, it's still relatively small and easier to get a decent property in. We bought a dual key property, which we'll talk about in more detail later. It's a cash positive property, but it's tax negative because of the depreciation schedules that we mentioned in Chapter Eight.

The next purchase was a commercial property which is subdividable into separate parts to allow for a higher rental yield, and I currently run my business out of one of the parts. This one was through our superannuation fund. The ones in America and Queensland are through my family trust, which we'll talk about in Chapter Twelve.

Our most recent purchase was an old, rundown house in Brisbane that's across two 405-square-metre blocks of land, each with its own title. Our plan is to build two houses on the blocks, sell one and keep one. Overall, we've got a spread of properties across five geographies – residential, commercial, units, houses and land.

This portfolio may not grow as fast as if we'd bought all of our properties in the same suburb that we were living in at the time in Sydney because that whole market went up 60% to 80% in the space of four years – something that's never been seen before. The same area is now down around 15% from the peak and still falling. Putting everything in one area is extremely risky, and ending up with massive growth or huge decline would be a matter of luck and timing. During the current decline, I'd be sitting at home depressed, as opposed to sitting on the shores of a lagoon in Vanuatu and enjoying the fruits of my diversified cash positive portfolio, while I write this.

How to raise funds

To get started with investing, the three main options are to save the first deposit, use a guarantor property as extra security, or get a short-term personal loan to cover deposit and costs. Once we're off and running, we can extract equity from any of our properties that go up in value, as well as continuing to save. We bought our first property when we were terrible at saving but knew I was about to get a bonus from work. Instead of waiting for the bonus, we put the deposit on credit card and then paid off the credit card debt when the bonus came in.

For our Phoenix properties, we took the difficult decision to sell our family home and use the surplus to buy cash positive investment properties. Our rent was similar to our previous mortgage, but it could be subsidised from the rental income we received.

As an alternative, more people are now looking to make partnerships or joint ventures with friends, as they realise that maybe one person has high income to help with servicing a loan and the other has a big deposit but a lower income. These partnerships can work well, but it's important to structure them appropriately to protect everyone's best interests. We funded one purchase via a mortgage from the vendor. All properly written up, but for them, the interest was a more stable income source than rent, due to high vacancies at that time.

For property, most of the funding is typically from banks, or other lenders, who like to lend around 80% for residential property, or around 70% for commercial.

It is possible to get 90% or 95% loans for residential and 80% for commercial properties. My ideal is 88%, which gives the highest relative return on our original deposits, by paying some mortgage insurance, but nowhere near as much LMI as the over-90% loans.

When we buy investment properties, we always add the expected rental income into the financials. For a construction, we assume the rent for the completed property, but we need to add the interest costs during construction phase as an additional cost.

As we saw from Rahul and Priya's example, banks will discount any rent we receive by 20% and assume we have to make principal and interest repayments at 6%. This will make even the most positively geared properties look negative and quickly eat into our surplus income as we build a portfolio.

ELEVEN

Portfolio Structure

In this chapter, we're going to look at strategically structuring a portfolio to balance the need for gains or for cash flow against the risks involved with owning property. A while ago, my wife and I were out with a big group and a friend of a friend who happened to be a financial planner had come along. He was obviously trying to assert his credentials and, not realising that there were any other qualified financial planners around, he said, 'Anyone who's got all their money in property is an idiot.' Kelly and I looked at each other, thinking, 'We've pretty much got all our money in property, but we'll let him go.' He then proceeded to tell the group about how it's important to diversify in different types of shares in different companies, in overseas shares and local shares, and with fixed cash assets and infrastructure, and so on, which is exactly what I was taught when I did my diploma in Financial Planning. In his head, property is one asset class, yet shares are many and varied.

Now, when it comes to property, which I prefer over shares, it's still important to diversify.

Unfortunately, too many people fall into a property portfolio where they own a house, then see an apartment in the next street for sale and buy it because they think it'll make a good investment property. Maybe the kids can move into it when they grow up. Then they see another one for sale and buy another one. They claim to have a portfolio of three properties, but they haven't actually built a portfolio. They've got three properties in the same location. When we borrow money to buy property, we are amplifying our gains and amplifying our losses. Great when the area grows, like we saw in Sydney from 2013–2017, but terrible from 2017–2019. Buying property with 90% loans means a 10% fall in the property value, and our loan is the same as our property value. If it falls further, we're in a negative equity position – worse off than if we'd never bought at all.

Instead, we need to structure a property portfolio in an intelligent way, designed to help support us long term and help balance each element. Most people are aware of the different property types, like apartments versus houses, but we're going to look at some of the other lesser-known property types in the following sections, such as dual income properties – like a house with a granny flat or commercial properties – as well as subdivisions or small lot subdivisions.

Location, location, location

We've all heard this in relation to property, but in this chapter we're going to take that quote quite literally, meaning it's important to have properties in at least three different locations. This will spread our risks of falls in property prices and increase our exposure to growth. We've spoken earlier about there being no such thing as 'the property market', but instead there are many small submarkets. Sydney is broken up into different regions and different property types, and then Melbourne is also broken into different regions and different property markets, which move at different times. The same for Brisbane, Perth and Adelaide, or any other capital city. Remember, nobody predicted the 60% to 80% jump in Sydney prices that happened from 2013 to 2017, but the signs were relatively good beforehand and now the signs are relatively gloomy. The signs are good in other regions in Australia and other parts of the world at the moment, if you've got access to them.

The other big consideration apart from the locations is property types. For example, units and houses tend to perform slightly differently. I'm not a big fan of units, simply because a change in planning permission could mean another giant block of units goes up next to it. Suddenly, our unit is no different than the brand-new ones that may have slightly better views, or slightly better fixtures and fittings. With a unit, all we own is a concrete box above ground somewhere, and the true value of the property is in the land content.

When clients of mine are saying that they want to buy an apartment, I always suggest that they look at the land content. To work that out, simply divide the total block of land that the complex is built on by the number of units. For some of the high rises with 100 apartments on 2,000 square metres, the land content is only 20 square metres (2,000/100 = 20), whereas an art-deco block might have four apartments on 300 square metres, which is 75 square metres each (300/4 = 75).

We also need to understand the difference between buying in a city and buying in the country. Unfortunately, people tend to assume that what happened in the city will eventually happen in the country, and that's simply not true. The value of land tends to go up with scarcity; they're not making more land close to the cities. The further we get from a city, the easier it is to divide up the next farm into a bunch of lots and make more land available. The further you get from the city centre, the more land is available, yet the fewer people want to live there, so the price is less likely to go up.

This applies even more in country areas, like Bathurst in New South Wales. Bathurst is a great little town, but it also has the benefit of having a hill that you can go to the top of and look down from and see the entire city. What you see is a very compact city, surrounded by a ridiculous amount of land. If we were going to buy a property in the area, why would it go up in value?

The other issue with country areas is that the populations tend to be relatively small and they fluctuate much more dramatically than in cities. In Australia, we have five cities of a million people or more, with 1% or 2% growth that tends to be steady over time due to migration and other factors. No single industry can dominate a city that size. By contrast, in the country somebody could open up a factory, or mine, and suddenly they need 5,000 extra workers in the area, so 5,000 people and their families need to move in. That means 5,000 houses need to get built, leading to a short-term shortage and rapid price rises. Once the extra houses get built and everyone's accommodated, then the prices may fall again or stabilise. Likewise, if an equivalent company in a country area shuts down, then we see the reverse effect. Suddenly there's a surplus of 5,000 houses, with very little natural population growth, so property prices fall because there's an abundance of them. I'm not a big fan of country areas, but if you know one that's got more than one thing going for it, then by all means, look at that area. Just be mindful of the fact that there is an abundance of land, especially in Australia.

The other part of my portfolio is, of course, the fact that I've got properties in multiple countries. I was able to do that partly because I was living in the UK when I bought over there and partly because I took cash to America and invested my cash over there when I was unable to get mortgages. You can get some mortgages in America as a foreigner, but they're very difficult to get and much more expensive than what you might see interest rates advertised for. If you do have the capability of buying in another country because of family or work, then by all means, go ahead. Keep in mind what the long-term play is going to be. Make sure you're not buying a cash negative property or a property that won't be able to service the loan if interest rates change.

The other thing I'd like to talk about regarding the location is the shares analogy. If we look at a portfolio of shares versus a portfolio of property, it's much more difficult to have 10 different properties in our portfolio in all different locations than it is to have 10 different shares, such as Woollies, Coles, BHP and Telstra. Shares can be diversified by industry, company or country relatively easily with relatively little money put towards each, whereas with property it's a much bigger amount of money so it's much more difficult to actually construct a portfolio, but it's still possible. We can spread the risk, and for most people anywhere between three and 10 properties will be enough to achieve our goals without going overboard.

Dual income for cash flow and capital gains

I love dual income properties. They're one of the best ways of getting what I call the best of both worlds in property, which is to buy something in a great location which normally is cash negative, but make it cash positive. We still get the long-term gains from an area that's likely to grow, while at the same time not spending money out of our own pocket to support that property. Dual income properties are also a great way of helping with borrowing capacity or at least stopping our borrowing capacity falling because the rents can be enough to cover the mortgages even if the interest rates go up.

There are a few different types of dual income properties; the most common one in Sydney is a house with a granny flat. In Sydney, we've got granny flat legislation, so if the block is more than 450 square metres, then we can get a private certifier to say it's okay to build a granny flat and we don't need to go through council planning. We should always check the regulations and talk to a private consultant, who will advise if and when we need to go to council. Rules are different in Queensland and Brisbane, where granny flats can't be rented separately from the main house.

As an example, Freddie bought a house for around $600,000, on a 500-square-metre block, that would rent for $450/week. He then spent $100,000 to build a granny flat and was suddenly able to collect $400/week on the flat but still get $450/week for the house. The granny flat was able to be separated by a fence, with rear-lane access, which is why the rent for the house was not impacted. $850/week on a $700,000 property is significantly better than $450/week on a $600,000 one.

Buying a house and a granny flat will typically cost a premium so he might have been able to sell for $700,000, but in Freddie's case, a bank valued his finished property at only $650,000. One of the downsides to owning a dual key is that if we go to sell or refinance them, there's not as many comparable sales for valuers to use.

The second type of dual income property, which is a similar concept to the first, is a Fonzie flat. These are usually custom built, and take their name from the old TV series *Happy Days*, where the Fonz used to live in a flat above the garage of the Cunningham family. I've got one of these up on the Sunshine Coast and it's configured as a three-bedroom house, with separate garage and carport. Above the garage and carport is a one-bedroom apartment. The carport is used by the apartment tenants, who can enter via their own stairs. The garage is used by the house tenants. The rent we get on the house is almost identical to the rent for standalone houses. The one-bedroom apartment, surprisingly, gets almost two thirds the rent of the house, so the overall yield is dramatically higher because of it.

One of the tricks with both a Fonzie flat and a granny flat is getting a separate electricity meter. Otherwise we have to pay all the electric bills for both tenants. On one block of land, there'll only be one water meter, so we have to pay for all of the water usage, but that's not normally a huge expense.

The more commonly understood dual income property is a duplex: two semidetached houses, joined in the middle on one block of land. They usually have mirrored floor plans, with garages side by side. It's cheaper to build a duplex than two standalone houses, but easier to get double the rent. Clients Paul and Helen are doing this in the Inner West, knocking down their old house on a big block of land. The duplex properties can be either sold off separately or Paul and Helen can live in one and rent the other. We really like the strategy for buying old houses on big blocks, building a duplex, selling off one of the two and keeping the other one in the portfolio. By selling off one, it's possible to cover most of the entry and deposit costs, get all of our money and sometimes a bit of profit, and still own a cash neutral or cash positive property.

Duplexes typically value much better than a house and granny flat or a Fonzie because people can see the value in the two dwellings side by side. It's possible to keep both on one rate's notice and one water rate until we're ready to sell. At that point we can get council approval to subdivide the two.

Subdivisions to accelerate capital growth

Subdivisions are a natural extension from duplexes. In their simplest form, we carve a big block into two, keeping the house and selling off the back or side yard. Alternatively, we can build on the vacant block and sell off the original house, or knock down the house and build two new ones. A small lot subdivision is a great way to make chunks of cash as opposed to generating income over the long run. They can also be used for cash flow over the long term, like with a duplex.

These small lot subdivisions can be side by side, if the block is wide enough, corner blocks or battle-axe. Councils normally have rules around minimum street frontages and driveways. Corner blocks let us build a house on one street frontage and the other house on the other street frontage. A battle-axe block has a side driveway by the house and then the back of the yard is cut off for another house. Our Brisbane property has a 20m-wide frontage, with 10m allowed per property, side by side.

There's also the Monopoly exception to the three-location rule – buy four green houses and replace with a red hotel. Freddie bought a rundown house on a decent block in Westmead, near a big hospital in western Sydney. Then he bought the property diagonally adjacent to his. He tried buying the other rear property and the one next door to complete the set of four, but he ended up agreeing to sell his two – as did the owners of the other two properties – to a developer. Each of them made more than double the prior value of the house. The developer was able to build an eight-storey block of units.

For more complex developments, the gains are potentially higher, the risks are higher and the level of sophistication required is higher. While tempting, it would be a bad idea to go too complex first off just because the gains look awesome, when what you really need to do is cut your teeth on a small lot subdivision before you go into a medium lot. Another client, Valerie, bought a three-bedroom house on 1,300 square metres, which was a relatively big block of land but not uncommon in the area. Due to a lot of development and investment in infrastructure, in an area of Brisbane called North Lakes, some of the surrounding suburbs got rezoned to allow townhouses to be built. On 1,300 square metres, eight townhouses can be built.

Once we go over two dwellings on a site, most banks will consider it as a commercial development. One or two lenders will allow four dwellings on one site, but more than four would always be commercial. For these, we need commercial finance, with a lot more calculations from an accountant to know our entry strategy, our holding costs and our exit strategy. There's a tremendous amount of risk with building eight townhouses. Firstly, in order to get planning permission, Valerie had to spend $40,000 or $50,000 and spend six to nine months with architects, surveyors, etc. The townhouses are going to cost about $180,000 each to build, or $1.44 million total. The existing house will have to be knocked down, so there will be no rental income until the townhouses are finished. A long-term developer, or someone with plenty of other funds at their disposal, might manage this comfortably. Going to a bank and saying, 'Can I borrow $1.9 million for a first-time development?' might not lead to a good outcome. A normal commercial loan is a little bit different to residential funding. We can only borrow about 60%–80% of the land plus construction cost.

The finished value might be $350,000 x 8 = $2.8m, but land plus construction value might be just $560,000 + $1.44m = $2m. Even at 80%, that's still only $1.6m, which is not enough to cover the funds needed for the construction and the initial loan, plus interest. The bank is also likely to ask for some presales, with a higher proportion expected for less-experienced developers. In other words, if Valerie's exit strategy is to sell six and keep two, well then she needs to have at least five buyers lined up. That would mean 5 x $350,000 = $1.65m, which would be enough to clear the $1.6m loan. That's what selling 'off the plan' means. In the case of commercial funding, there's no serviceability/borrowing capacity issues with a good exit strategy.

Valerie needs $1.44m for the construction, plus $360,000 to cover her initial loan and another $100,000 to cover interest costs during construction = $1.9m. If $1.6m is the maximum based on 80% of $2m, she will need another $300,000. Getting more funding from somewhere else to make it work is called 'mezzanine finance'. This can be done with a second, higher-cost short-term lender, by providing additional property as security, borrowing from family, or finding an equity partner who will make up the shortfall in return for a share of the profits.

These projects have the most potential for gain, but also the biggest risks. Valerie capitalised on an opportunity because the planning guidelines changed to allow townhouses in the area. Others did the same, so it means quite a few townhouses are being built, which means the price of townhouses has come off slightly.

For these types of subdivisions, banks want to see 20% profit, or a bare minimum 15%, as further price falls put their money at risk. The worst-case scenario is to get halfway through a project and run out of money to finish the build. People that buy off the plan may sign contracts to buy at $350,000, but if the price falls, they may not be able to get their finance to settle on the loan. They may lose their 10% deposit, but until Valerie gets paid for each property, she's paying interest on the construction loan, so nobody wants a delay.

If that wasn't enough to scare you off, then the next level up is major subdivisions. This is where we buy multiple acres in an area that we can subdivide into 10, 20, 30 or more lots. The profits are phenomenal on these, but you need experience, great financial backing and a great accountant to make this all work for you so that you can actually see the gains through, which might take several years. People sometimes buy land in an area which is likely to have a zonal change at some point in the future, but that zonal change might take years to come through, or never eventuate.

It's tempting to think: 'A $1 million block of land is now worth $5 million if developed, so why not sell the whole thing to a developer for $5 million?' A developer has to have services connected like water and electric, get roads connected, and make sure there's adequate drainage and green areas. Spending $5m on land plus another $1m–$2m on infrastructure might take a number of presales before the developer can go ahead with it. A developer is far more likely to pay a modest gain on the original block to keep funds available for the infrastructure work, so it's highly unlikely they will pay $5m for the block. To make that sort of return, we'd need to do the development ourselves.

Subdivisions are great ways of making chunks of money, quite quickly. They're also great ways of, for example, buying a lot which has eight dwellings and keeping two or four of them or buying a lot which has the capacity for twenty dwellings and keeping four or five but selling off the rest to pay down the debts. But the risks are tremendous, and you need a lot of careful planning and research as well as a very strong stomach.

Commercial properties

I think commercial properties are a great way of diversifying a portfolio. Commercial properties do tend to behave very differently to residential ones, and therefore even within a market like Sydney, we find that commercial properties will grow at different paces in different directions to residential properties, even though they might be next to one another. There is always the long-term prospect of starting off as commercial and becoming residential later on.

There are a few different types of commercial property. One of the biggest groups is offices. Offices are a bit like apartments in that they sit in strata blocks.

There are the same risks with apartments: a new office block can go up, and that will decimate the value of all the offices in the area. Offices can have surprisingly good returns, though, providing you've got a tenant. This is one of the biggest problems with commercial property versus residential. If we get the rent right on an apartment, it'll rent in under a month on a six- to twelve-month lease. Commercial properties can be vacant for months at a time, but the upside is that tenants can sign up for one, three or five years. It's important to understand the rental market for the property type we buy and the availability of similar properties, and price accordingly.

Another thing to be aware of with commercial versus residential is: typically, the tenant pays the outgoings. So, you can get them to pay rates, water rates, strata – anything you can write into a contract that the tenant signs. They'll pay to gut the property, to renovate it, to do all sorts of stuff to the inside because it's what they need to make the property work for their business. A business doesn't want to rock up, put all their office furniture in, and build their reception desk and get all their equipment in, and then six months later move on to another premises. You'll often hear terms like 'three plus three' or 'five plus five', which means the tenant will sign a lease for five years, with an option to extend for another five. Rental increases might be built into the contract, with a review versus the market at the changeover from the first five to the second five years.

It's important to remember that bad tenants still exist for commercial properties, ones who hit financial difficulties and stop paying the rent. Worst case, they close the doors and wind up their business, putting us in the queue with a line of other creditors asking to get our rent paid.

Good offices, in good locations that are well maintained and well managed, can give us a great yield – 7% is currently quite typical. There are great commercial loans on 75% of the value of the property at rates that are quite similar to those of investment home loans, or around 5%.

Shops are another big category of commercial properties. These can be single shopfront or a shop with offices or residence above. They will be treated as commercial even though there's a residence involved that we might choose to live in. Again, the trick is finding and retaining a good tenant with a good business model that will stay in place for a long time. Otherwise, a lot of retail businesses come in and rent shops and then go out of business quickly. We often see a lot of shopfronts vacant, and they can be vacant for quite some time until an area goes through regeneration, or the right business comes in and takes it on.

Factories can be great investments and are typically in industrial or semi-industrial areas. The property might not necessarily hold a factory; it might be just used as a warehouse. The yields can be great, as with offices, and tenants are more likely to be long-term, with lower failure rates than a shop. Lots of people think they can open up a shop but not many people think they can manufacture unless they spend a lot of money on equipment and have a lot of knowledge in a specific area and have had a go in their garage first. Factories can also be quite good long-term plays when an area changes from, or is in the process of changing from, industrial to residential. Suddenly, we can go from getting commercial rents and commercial values to residential values, which can be considerably higher.

The office that I bought in Sydney is a 98-square-metre space with a rear-lane shopfront. It has a kitchen, toilet and shower room, and it has multiple rooms broken up within it. It could at some point in the future become an apartment, and at 98 square metres would be quite a decent sized one. But because it was commercial, in an area that had been vacant for quite some time, I picked it up for half the price of an 80-square-metre apartment selling in the same block. Half price just because one is commercial and the other residential, and that might change in the future.

There are many other property types under the commercial umbrella, like petrol stations, small holdings and child care centres, but too many to cover in great detail here – and, aside from child care centres, I don't have as much experience with them to share.

176

Property is not one generic asset type, and it's important to consider the different types and locations when building a portfolio. There are lots of elements which are easy to access and look at – we can think outside of the square. We're much more likely to make a decent yield in a decent area or be able to make chunks of cash if we do things that others don't. Of course, buying a mixture of different types of properties in different locations also diversifies our portfolio.

When investing overseas makes sense

I own property in the UK and the US, so I often get asked about investing overseas and if now is a good time to buy in this market or that market.

The simple answer is that it's much easier to buy property in the country you are living in than anywhere overseas. In Chapter Ten, we showed that borrowing to buy is what makes property outperform shares. I bought in the UK when I was living there and earning an income to use for servicing my mortgages. This meant I was able to put very little of my own funds in to own three investment properties. Borrowing more to buy over there is much more difficult now, as I'd need a UK bank to accept my Australian tax returns as evidence of income. The interest rates would also be higher than borrowing as a local.

The same is true in the US, where I predominantly bought with funds from Australia. It is possible to get mortgages over there, but I was unable to in Arizona. Banks over here won't lend against overseas securities, so the loans need to be arranged where the property is. There were many more complexities to buying over there than I realised. I knew about the basics of avoiding areas with long-term population decline, which were the properties advertised for under $10,000. I knew that I had to set up a US company to be able to own property, so I did that fairly easily. I didn't realise that property managers over there are massively different to here or the UK. I got scammed by an agent, who had so many hidden fees, both for landlord and tenant, that they made most of their money from dodgy fees. Their modus operandi was getting in terrible tenants and then charging landlords a fortune to get rid of them, to go to court, pay their internal maintenance team to work on the property, etc. After six months of receiving no rent from them at all, they tried to sue me for $10,000 in fees. Thankfully, I switched to a better agent and got rid of the bad one without paying their huge bill or ending up in court.

Any long-distance relationship can be challenging at times, so finding and working with property agents is critical. With good agents, I get lots of photos before and after any work is done. They do regular property inspections and rent reviews. The best ones suggest improvements that add value to the property. My US agent recently recommended we turn a huge two-bedroom, one-bathroom apartment with a shared laundry into a three-bedroom, two-bathroom apartment with an internal laundry. We were able to increase the rent by 33% and will get back our investment in remodelling in under three years.

My recommendation for overseas property is to only buy in good areas with population growth and only when you can borrow to buy, or while living there, or with really close family ties to that country.

In any case, the bigger the portfolio and the more you borrow, the bigger the risks, so maybe we should look at breaking down the ownership into smaller chunks before looking at managing those risks.

TWELVE

Ownership Structures

Most people start out wondering if they're going to invest in their own name, their partner's name or together. But there's actually a lot more to ownership structures, especially if you want to build a portfolio over the long run. In this chapter, we're going to take you through some of the different ownership structures. Firstly, we'll look at owning a property jointly or together with someone, and what sort of percentages you can use. I'll take you through my own family trust, why we have it and how it works. We'll also look at family trusts and discretionary trusts in general and the benefits of those. Then we'll look at unit trusts, which are less frequently used for property, but they do have their uses in certain cases. Lastly, we'll examine self-managed superfund – or SMSF – ownership, because I often get asked whether people should be buying a property in their superannuation fund. There's some basics to understand before that's even an appropriate question.

Different structures are more suitable, at different times, for some people than others. Over the long run, to build a portfolio, it's more likely that you'll get involved in the more advanced structures. So, let's get stuck into it.

Why together and joint are different

David and Ellie were planning their life together, but still not married or living together, and wanted to buy. The simplest type of property ownership is 'sole ownership', which means one person owns 100% of the property. Sole ownership could have been possible for David, but his borrowing power would have been much lower than it was together with Ellie, and she had neither enough savings nor enough income to buy on her own.

The next simplest option for them is 'joint tenants', which is when you buy property together with someone. Technically, you own the property jointly, and that means that each one of you owns 100% of the property. If it's an investment property, then it will be treated as 50/50 ownership. But in the event of, for example, one of you passing away, then the other one owns the 100%. There is nothing for the person who's passed away to leave to anyone else because the property is owned by the other joint tenant. This would be a risk for David and Ellie, if they were to split up and then one of them died. The survivor would own the property and the family of the deceased partner would have no claim on it.

Joint tenancies can be quite convenient for married couples, and in some circumstances between parents and their children. If parents own property jointly with their children, when they pass away the children automatically own the property without having to go through probate. Likewise, if one spouse dies, the other owns the property.

The other way of buying property together with someone is called 'tenants in common'. This could be with a partner, sibling, friend or anyone else, but you own the property in specified shares. The simplest form is 50/50, which means that each one of you individually owns half the property. If something happens in the relationship or one of you passes away, then the half that person owned gets passed onto whomever is in the person's will.

It's horrible to talk about dying, but we have to think about these eventualities. With tenants in common, we can nominate any percentage ownership – 60/40, 70/30, even 99/1. This became the perfect solution for

David and Ellie: as David had a bigger deposit and higher income, we calculated that he could afford 60% of the property and Ellie could afford the other 40%. The mortgages were separated so that they each knew what their costs were and each reflected the size of their respective contributions. They were also confident that, if the relationship didn't last, they were each protected from any disagreements about the purchase. As it turns out, they ended up marrying and later merged their loans into one, but at least they had peace of mind to buy in the first place.

Joint tenancies can also be used for tax purposes, to weight the ownership in favour of one person in a couple – for example, 99/1. However, with the low percentage shares, some banks won't recognise a less than 10% and sometimes a less than 20% ownership as being high enough to be involved in the loan. A good broker can find ways of getting around different bank rules, and a good solicitor should explain the different structures to you.

Overall, we can use joint tenancies quite strategically with family members, but we would tend to recommend tenants in common for more situations than joint tenancies, which is more or less for married couples and also long-term properties where there's no concern with taxation.

My family trust

Hassle Free Life Services is a company that I set up when I was first starting out in business, but we later neutralised the company and then used it as a trustee for our family trust. It's generally advisable to start a new company for a trust, though. We bought our first few investment properties in joint names, but realised over time that because we tend to buy cash flow positive properties, profits get split 50/50. Half of the profits automatically get added to my income regardless of what tax bracket I'm in, relative to Kelly.

Trust income has to be distributed to beneficiaries each year, but we have to decide where to allocate that profit. We can allocate income to the person earning the lowest income because they're going to pay less tax. I recommend speaking to an accountant, who can help with splitting the income each year. The other consideration is that we've now got adult children and so we can actually allocate the profits according to the trust deed to anybody that my wife and I are related to. Kelly and I are named beneficiaries, but our accountant can allocate profits to our children, brothers, sisters, fathers, mothers, etc., as well as any education establishments any of us attend. We can split the profits between whoever's got the lowest income in the family rather than just between the two of us.

With property ownership, we ultimately want to be able to make money to support ourselves in retirement. People often make the mistake of focusing on the short term – for example, buying a property as tenants in common, 90/10 in favour of the person on the highest income because of negative gearing benefits. The problem gets reversed once the property is making money, either because rents have gone up or because we've paid the mortgage down. Then 90% of the profits get allocated to the higher income earner.

My focus has always been on retirement, so we know we can split the income between us, through our family trust.

The other reason for setting up a trustee company is because we are self-employed and use the trust to own shares in our business. This means we can allocate profits from the company to the trust, which can then distribute those profits according to whomever makes the most sense. The trustee company is the shareholder of the overseas company that owns our US properties, too. Any money we make from overseas flows back through to our family trust, and that enables us to share the profits out from there.

How to use family trusts

There are a number of elements to understand in a family trust or discretionary trust. Firstly, we have trustees. The trustees are the ones responsible for the overall ownership of the trust, and we can have individual trustees (including a solicitor) or a company as trustee. These are separate to the beneficiaries, who are the people who get the benefits from the trust. For example, I could be a trustee of a discretionary trust and my kids could be beneficiaries of that trust. I would get to decide what goes on and sign any paperwork, but my kids are the beneficiaries, so they'll get paid. In my will, I might specify that a solicitor take over as trustee if I die. When you hear about trust fund babies, they are normally the beneficiaries of a wealthy family member's estate.

Trusts can also make losses, but those losses are carried forward, rather than being allocated to an individual to use like negative gearing. If a trust makes a loss this year, it gets carried forward to next year. If the trust makes a loss again, the combined losses get carried forward and then eventually when the trust makes a profit, the trust doesn't have to allocate that profit until all of the previous losses have been absorbed.

The trustee, or director of the trustee company, will also determine if there's more beneficiaries than just the named beneficiaries. So, a discretionary or family trust often will have Mum and Dad as trustees, and Mum and Dad as beneficiaries of the trust, but additional beneficiaries could include anybody that they're related to. The trust deed might specify, parents, children, siblings and grandchildren, or it could include cousins and uncles and aunts and grandparents and any other type of beneficiary.

Standard trust deeds can be downloaded from the internet for around $100, with a standard list of related beneficiaries and an extra line for education establishments attended by the beneficiaries – potentially a great way to pay school fees.

If we can allocate the profits year to year, we can potentially reduce our tax liability. Rather than property being all in the name of the higher income earner, we could allocate the money to the lower income earner who pays less tax, or to somebody in the family who pays no tax at all. It's important to note that we cannot get a negative gearing benefit through a family trust. There needs to be other profits coming into that family trust which can be offset by the negative gearing property.

From a lending perspective, an investment property in the name of a family trust, which has a corporate trustee, is not covered under the National Consumer Credit Protection Act. Therefore, a lot of the big banks will deem it a commercial transaction. They may still give us residential interest rates, but they will assess it differently to a residential transaction. Sometimes the interest rates aren't as attractive. Sometimes they are just as good. Sometimes you can get better serviceability, or greater borrowing capacity, through the trust than if it was through the individuals.

Family trusts can also own shares in a company and multiple properties, but we might also choose to set up a new family trust for a new property. In some states, like Queensland, each company, or corporate trustee, has its own land tax allowance. This means once one company has used up its land tax allowance, we can buy the next property through a different one. In NSW, companies and family trusts have no land tax allowance. The more complex we get, the more costs we have in setting up the trust and ongoing costs. Typically, accountants will help set them up, sometimes solicitors, and then there are ongoing maintenance issues. A family trust must submit a tax return every year, which accountants charge for, and a corporate trustee must pay an annual fee to ASIC (the Australian Securities and Investments Commission) each year, currently around $250.

Another potential benefit of a family trust is separation of ownership. If we had a company that goes belly up, then creditors can seize assets from the company, or you as an individual, but they can't necessarily seize assets that are owned in the trust. Likewise, if you're in a high litigation profession such as doctor, lawyer or financial planner, where you have the risk of getting sued, family trust assets may be protected. There are various ways of unwinding and unpicking the trust if you've deliberately done something that's dodgy, but that's something you should take up with a solicitor or accountant.

Two of our staff members just bought their first investment properties interstate, so elected to use newly set-up family trusts. These give them long-term flexibility, but because they are not buying in their own names, they are not discounted from FHB concessions in the future.

Unit trusts

Family trusts and unit trusts have similar structures of separate beneficiaries and trustees, but the difference between a unit trust and a family trust is that each unit holder has a fixed percentage benefit. For example, with two people, it could be 50% for one person and 50% for the other person that's fixed. These are really only beneficial if buying with non-family members. The unit trust means everyone knows what their share is going to be.

Coming back to the example of Valerie's development, to secure the extra funds she could set up a unit trust together with her sister to do the development together. Each could be unit holders, and maybe eight units could be issued, corresponding to the eight townhouses to be built. Valerie could have six units and her sister two. The trust deed could specify that at the end of the build each unit holder gets a townhouse.

SMSFs

A self-managed superfund (SMSF) is a type of unit trust that complies with the superannuation act. In simple terms, let's say Sam and Joe are looking at buying a property and they ask if they can buy it in their superannuation fund. Well, they can, but the superannuation fund is like a third person. So now we have Sam, Joe and the SMSF. If we want to borrow, then we look at the assets and income of that SMSF, not necessarily of Sam or Joe. The assets comprise how much money is built up in the SMSF. The income may be the rent from the property that they're looking to buy, and also 9.5% of Sam's income and 9.5% of Joe's income because that's the amount automatically going to the fund from their salaries.

Sam and Joe can still be guarantors and they can still offer to contribute more to their superfund than the minimum. That means their income is at risk and they will have to make repayments on the loan, should they be required. Like a unit trust, the ultimate ownership is always the percentage share according to whatever Sam and Joe have put in. If Sam put in 10% and Joe put in 90% of the fund, Sam is entitled to 10% of the benefits and Joe is entitled to 90%.

An SMSF can have up to four beneficiaries. The beneficiaries and the trustees have to be the same people if they're individuals; or, if it's a corporate trustee, then each one of them has to be a director of the trustee company. They're all liable for whatever happens to that fund – and also liable for making sure that the fund stays compliant with the regulations. The best thing to do if you want to create an SMSF is speak to your accountant, and often a financial planner will help set these up. If we draw any funds out of the superfund before we're old enough, then we've broken the law. The tax penalties can be quite huge. On the other hand, superannuation funds are a great way of parking funds and owning property, especially cash positive properties where we don't need to draw any of those funds off until we retire.

We can't live in an SMSF property, or derive a benefit from it – for example, as a weekender, rented for part of the year and used as a holiday home for the rest. Loans are around 2% more expensive than any other property loans, and normally 20%–30% deposit is required.

Why so few properties are owned by companies

It is possible to just set up a company to buy property, either to keep or onsell. The company has shareholders who can get the benefit of any profits, as distinct from one or more directors, who make the decisions for the company.

The upsides of owning property through a company are that the tax rate is lower, currently at 27.5%, and that taxed profits can stay within the company, without needing to be taxed further. They could then be spread out over multiple years to help smooth out the individual tax costs. If profits are distributed to shareholders, they would most likely be fully franked, so the shareholders would have to pay their tax rate on the grossed up amount and then get credit back for the tax already paid.

The downside to owning through a company is that the distributions are fixed by shareholding, a bit like a unit trust. To change the shareholding from one person to two would require a transfer of shares, which could trigger CGT. Should the property be sold, any capital gain would be fully taxed at 27.5%, whereas individuals can currently get a 50% discount on the amount of capital gain that gets taxed. For example, if a property were sold with a $100,000 capital gain, the company would pay $27,500 in tax, and if that gain were distributed to shareholders they might need to pay additional tax on top. A $100,000 gain made by an individual or allocated to an individual via a trust, on the other hand, would be reduced to $50,000 and then taxed. For these reasons, companies are rarely used as vehicles for individuals and families to hold property long term.

With all the best intentions, though, things can still go wrong, and it's time to look at how to manage those risks.

THIRTEEN

Risk Management

In this chapter, we're going to look at the risks associated with having a property portfolio because the more we own, the more we owe and the higher the probability that something will go wrong.

We'll walk you through a risk worksheet that we use with our clients and some of the things that we look at with them. We'll also look at when to fix interest rates to reduce risk in our portfolios. In the last section, we'll look at how much of a buffer to carry to manage the risks. So, let's have a look at the risk worksheet.

How to assess risk

We always start off risk assessment by drawing a vertical line down the centre of the page and looking at the risks on the left side of the page. It's important to explore all the things that are bothering us or holding us back. Write down all of those risks first – or at least think of them as you look at the table below.

Risks	
Individual:	
Property:	
External:	

The first set of risks we'll look at is the risks to the individual, then the risks to the property itself and what can go wrong. Finally, we'll go through the external risks, before we look at solutions.

Risks	
Individual:	
Redundancy	
Illness/injury	
Pregnancy	
Relationship	
Property:	
Unexpected repairs	
Bad tenant	
No tenant	
Accident, natural disaster, etc.	
External:	
Market fall	
Interest rates rise	
Increased living cost	

Once the list has been completed with all the risks, we can look at the solutions for each.

Risks	Solutions
Individual:	
Redundancy	?
Illness/injury	Income protection
Pregnancy	?
Relationship	Legal advice
Property:	
Unexpected repairs	?
Bad tenant	Landlord's insurance
No tenant	?
Fire/flood, etc.	Landlord's insurance
External:	
Market fall	Research/buyer's agent
Interest rates rise	Consider fixed rates
Increased living cost	Budget management

The '?' items can all be solved with a single word: 'Buffer'. With an adequate buffer, we can ride out a temporary loss of income through redundancy, pregnancy or vacancy. We can also cover unexpected repairs.

When to fix interest rates

If we fix the interest rates, we are actually fixing three things:

1. **The interest rate**. That could be a good or a bad thing. People often make the mistake of comparing the current fixed rates with the current variable rate and say, 'Oh, there's a saving' or 'It's more expensive' or whatever. But the reality is we're fixing the rate for a period of time and therefore the variable interest rate today is not relevant. What's relevant is what the interest rate might be in the future.

2. **The fixed rate term**. In Australia, fixed rate terms are typically one, three and five years, although we can also get two, four, six or seven years, or longer. But banks in Australia tend to trade money in one-, three- and five-year buckets, so those tend to be the most economical interest rate points. If you need to break that fixed rate to refinance, then the bank will sting you for break costs. The easiest way to think about break costs is to imagine the bank as buying and selling money. Let's say they buy money at 2% from depositors who put money in the bank, guaranteed for the next, say, three years. If the bank onsells that money to you for 4%, then they know they're making a guaranteed 2% profit on the way through. If a year later you needed to sell the property, the bank has already committed to pay

2% to the people they borrowed from in the first place, so now they've got to resell that money to someone else. If interest rates have risen so they can now get 5% interest on that money instead of 4%, the bank will be happy to take the money back and there'll be no break fee. But if interest rates have fallen to, let's say, 3%, then they're going to sting you for the difference. That's two years remaining at 1%. On a $500,000 loan, the break fee would be $10,000. We can't actually calculate break fees until we're ready to break because they depend on what the interest rates are at that point in time. Generally speaking, we only want to fix for as far forward as we can see that we're not going to sell or refinance.

3. **The loan amount.** Let's say we borrow $500,000 fixed for three years and then suddenly come into some money through inheritance or sale of another property or a bonus, and we want to pay extra off the loan or put money into an offset account linked to that loan. The bank's going to treat that a bit like breaking the rate, because we're giving them money back that they now need resell to someone else. Most banks set limits on how much extra we can pay against the loan and won't allow an offset, although there are a couple of exceptions.

We always want the flexibility to be able to pay extra onto a loan or have an offset account. We would therefore have at least one variable loan and then consider fixing the others. As we build up a property portfolio, we're more likely to fix the additional property and for a longer period of time – say, five years. That way we know the return, based on rent versus the fixed rate.

We use fixing as a risk management tool. Let's think back to Tom and Sarah from Chapter Six. We mentioned that a 2% interest rate increase on $500,000 would cost $10,000/year. For Sarah on $100,000, the risk is much higher than for Tom on $180,000, so Sarah might consider fixing half of the loan, whereas Tom could keep it all variable. If Tom bought an investment property and borrowed another $500,000, the risk of a 2% rate rise would grow to $20,000. Even though his income would grow by around $20,000/year from rent, $20,000 would still be a big hit to his total income of $200,000. He could keep the first property loan as variable and fix the second one. Should we build a property portfolio and end up with $2 million in debt, a 2% interest rate rise would cost $40,000 a year. Fixing would then be an essential part of the mix.

Essentially, the more we owe relative to income, the more we fix, but it does depend on our appetite for risk. If we like to live life on the edge, we might keep more variable, but if we're more conservative we would fix more. With a portfolio, it's also prudent to avoid fixing everything for the same period at the same time. If we fix the whole portfolio for five years, we run the bigger risk that five years from now our entire portfolio is suddenly going to become variable. If interest rates go up in that period of time, we're going to have a problem, in terms of both trying to refinance or get a better deal. It's better to take some of the loans over three years and some of them over five years, or fix some for five years this year and fix another one for five years next year and another one for five years the year after. The best thing to do is sit down and work this out with your broker to find the best solution for you.

How big is my buffer?

Buffering is one of the most important things we need to do to give ourselves peace of mind as investors. That means it's a bad idea to put every cent into the next property and then find that we've got nothing left in the tank to cover any urgent problems. In reality, how much of a buffer do we need?

The answer to that question depends on what stage we're up to and our ability to save money and rebuild our buffer. As a general rule of thumb, the bare minimum that we need is a month's worth of expenses – enough to cover the mortgage repayments on the investment loans, plus any rates and strata and water rates. We need at least that much in case there's a delay on rent coming in, or a vacancy. But we also need enough to cover unexpected repairs, which could stretch to another couple of months' worth.

We recently decided to renovate one property. As I mentioned before, there was an opportunity to convert a two-bedroom apartment into a three-bedroom apartment by splitting up one of the huge living room areas. It took longer than we expected. The guy that was doing the work was busy doing something else by the time the tenant got out, and then everything was held up again because they found some issues with the plumbing and wiring when they got into it. That blew the costs out a little bit more, and it meant that we were not only without the rent but we were also paying a higher cost for those renovations at the time. Ideally, six months' worth of expenses would have covered that less stressfully.

We're most comfortable in our lives when we're sitting on a two-year buffer. That means we can cover all our expenses related to our property and our own personal living expenses for two years. That includes a sustained period where we might have a combination of repairs for a property, vacancies and maybe a temporary loss of income.

I used to be with another franchise system, one which went belly up in 2011, and the administrators that moved in said that they wouldn't pay any commissions for anything that happened prior to that day. My income dropped to zero for three flat months. Without our buffer, everything would have fallen apart. I also know friends that have lost their jobs and taken a year to get back into the workforce at a level to which they're comfortable and happy. Two years' buffer gives you an enormous sense of security. We normally keep those funds in an offset, or redraw.

Stage Four: Portfolio summary

Property can be a great way to accelerate our path to retirement, especially when we borrow to do it. But a property portfolio has to be balanced by city, type and strategy to give us the greatest exposure to gain and the least risk of collapses. Experienced investors rarely hold much property in their own name, and family trusts offer tremendous flexibility.

If we can't manage risks, then we shouldn't be investing in property at all and will probably be reluctant to dive in. Write down as many risks as you can think of and then buy all the insurances you can.

Use fixed rates to insure against rate rises and then keep as big a buffer as you can to cover everything else that can't be insured. Beyond that, we're better off paying down the loans, which is what we're going to look at in the next stage.

Pay off owner-occupied debt first. The rates might look lower than those of other debts, but when we calculate the tax differences we're normally better off getting rid of it. Then we can knock over the other debts using 50% of our income, instead of only 20%.

STAGE FIVE

PAY DOWN

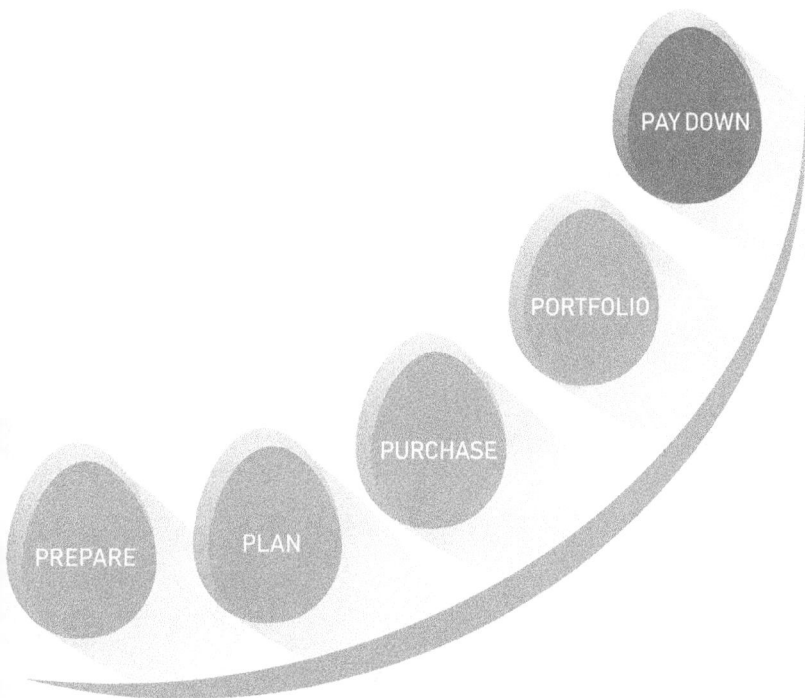

FOURTEEN

Eliminate Risk

Pay Down is the fifth strategically important step of any planned property portfolio. It's one that can be overlooked or taken up a little bit too enthusiastically at too early a stage. Our aim is to explain how to pay down debt strategically to reduce risk, how debt reduction is part of our exit plan and why knowing what your end game looks like is so important.

There are people that believe, or spruik, that you can buy ten properties, wait till they double in value, sell five and pay off the debt from the other five. There's a small element of truth in that simplistic assumption, but it's a highly risky strategy. The reality is that we should be able to pay off any debt we take on, without necessarily selling properties or assuming any property market is going to double in a reasonable timeframe.

After addressing that issue, we will look at how we can reduce the risks of gearing in property and specifically how paying off our non-deductible debt will be the first priority.

Next, we'll look at how to maintain flexibility, both in terms of being able to adapt to changing markets and circumstances and to increase our probability of success. Then we'll look at a case study of a client who did something that makes no sense on the face of it but was a perfect solution for them, taking into account their long-term needs.

Pay off non-deductible debt

Non-deductible debt is the debt on our long-term family home, for which we cannot claim a tax deduction. Paying off our home is one of the most important things we can do.

Recently, we've had more and more clients who are hung up on interest rates. Harry, a long-term client with three properties, said his owner-occupied loans had a 3.8% interest rate and his most expensive investment debt was at 4.8%. Since 4.8% is the most expensive, he suggested paying it off first or linking his offset to the 4.8% debt. You've probably guessed that he's wrong, but maybe aren't sure why, so let's take a step back. In order to pay the owner-occupied debt, Harry has to earn money, pay tax and then pay the interest. For the investment debt, he earns money, pays interest and then pays tax. Harry earns over $90,000 and his tax rate is 39%, so let's look at the two options side by side in the table below. We will assume he can move $100,000 from one offset account to another, to change the interest bill.

	Own home	investment
Interest rate	3.8%	4.8%
Interest on $100k	$3,800	$4,800
Income needed	$6,230	$4,800
Tax paid 39%	$2,530	$0
Net available	$3,800	$4,800
Effective rate	6.23%	4.8%

Below is a table showing the equivalents for the other tax brackets.

Tax Bracket	Gross Equivalent Needed to Pay 3.8%
21.5% ($18.2k–37k)	4.84%
34.5% ($37–87k)	5.8%
39% ($87k–180k)	6.23%
47% (>$180k)	7.17%

It's important to reduce the non-deductible debt but then make sure we reduce the debt burden on our homes. We're talking about the long-term family home. Just because we live in a place doesn't necessarily mean we should try to make that debt go away, in case it could be an investment in the future. When David and Ellie from Chapter Four were living in a two-bedroom apartment during life stage number two, they kept as much money as possible in an offset account. This put them in a stronger position to buy a bigger house and enabled them to more quickly pay that down. Not only does it reduce their costs, it also reduces their risk. The smaller the debt on their own home, the smaller the risk of losing it during a major economic downturn. Ideally, with no debt on their family home, a bank would be unable to repossess that property to recover debts on their investment property. Having no debt means the property is unencumbered, and hopefully we can get there quickly.

While paying off the non-deductible debt, we should seriously consider paying interest only on all the investment loans. Once we've paid off the family home, then there will be a lot more funds available to pay off debts on the other properties.

From Chapter Two, we learned that living rent free should increase savings to 50% of income. The assumption at the time was living with parents, but it applies equally to those who have paid off their family home. It's amazing how fast we can knock off our investment debts when it costs nothing to live in our own home.

First, we focus on either paying down the debt on the property we live in or building up an offset account if it's not our long-term family home and paying interest only. There are strategic ways to pay principal and interest with a line of credit, which we mentioned in Chapter Nine; but otherwise pay interest only on the investment or potential investment properties.

Maintain flexibility

Maintaining flexibility is a key part of a long-term investment strategy. That means that if we think a property could be an investment property in the future, even though we're currently living in it, then we're much better off building up an offset account rather than paying down the debt. If we paid down the debt from, say, $500,000 to $300,000, and then decided to move out and use it as an investment property, the bank might allow us to take the extra $200,000 as 'redraw'. But the tax office will say that the $200,000 is for a different purpose, namely to buy another home to live in. Therefore, the $200,000 redraw is not tax deductible against the investment property. If we put the $200,000 into an offset account, then while we're living in the property the bank will charge us interest on the $300,000 that we owe, but we can take that $200,000 as a deposit for our next home, and interest on the full $500,000 would remain deductible. Keeping funds in the offset account gives us that flexibility to move between properties. Redraw will do the same thing if it's a long-term family home, and any future redraw to buy an investment property will become deductible to that.

As we pay down the debt, we need to have the ability to redraw the surplus funds to maintain flexibility in managing our finances. We never know when we're going to need more money to do some renovations or repairs, cover a shortfall of rent, or be able to cope with a personal disaster or a period of unemployment. Being able to take those funds back again is absolutely critical to having a robust strategy. If a loan doesn't have a redraw facility, or offset, then every dollar we pay off is gone and we can't get it back again without putting in a new application. Then we run the risk of having no buffer funds available to cover any eventuality.

The $1m offset for true freedom

A great little case study we have is from a client of ours, Jane. Jane had raised a family in the outer suburbs, but after a divorce and the kids growing up she was on her own, with too big a home to manage. It didn't fit with the lifestyle that she wanted to lead, spending more time going out and enjoying time with friends in the city. When she was buying, Jane hadn't sold her family home. There was a slight difference in the cost and some renovations to the new place, which would leave her with about $100,000 worth of debt to buy in the city. Most people would have just borrowed $100,000 and tried to pay that off ASAP. Instead of doing that, we suggested that she borrow $1 million to buy before she sold, and afterwards she would have surplus funds of approximately $900,000. After a year or two, she ended up with $1m in her offset account and no interest to pay. This bought her a massive amount of flexibility.

A few years later, Jane was made redundant with no redundancy pay out because she was a contractor. Suddenly she was out of work, and it wasn't easy to find new employment. Employers tend to be biased against people over 50, and it took Jane two years to find another job. That huge offset account gave her the flexibility to maintain her lifestyle and cover her costs. Although she increased her non-deductible debt during that time, she's still got time to pay that down before retirement.

We never know what life is going to throw at us, and imagine a situation where Jane had to sell other assets or try and dip into superannuation. Without the $1m offset, she might have had to sell her home or give up her city lifestyle. No bank would have given her a loan while she wasn't working. Having the flexibility of her offset account made a dramatic difference in Jane's life.

Build up as much money as possible in redraw or offset, and $1m in cash would be lovely to have on hand, just in case.

FIFTEEN

Exit Plan

Our exit plan is knowing how we're going to end up once we don't have to work for money. We need to know how to pay down any remaining debts, what we're going to live on and how much we need to retire. In this chapter, first we'll look at the statistics behind retirement and the depressingly low number of people who fund their own retirement. We're hoping that we can inspire you to fund yours. The next thing to consider is how long we might live and what quality of life we might have for some of that time. It's important that we don't just cover ourselves for the first five years of retirement but can fund a long retirement.

Ultimately, no matter how much we might try and look after ourselves, we are going to depart this world, so it's important to have a legacy plan in place and know how our children, grandchildren, other family members, and everyone else who's important to us is going to cope without us. Let's get into the exit plan.

Retirement reality

There are currently 3.8 million Australians over 65, or 15% of the country's population.[2] Around 3 million of those receive a full or partial pension. At 65, men can expect to live another 20 years and women another 22 years.[3]

Despite the above statistics, everyone I speak to under 30 wants to retire by age 50, which would mean 35 years in retirement, on average. The old age pension for a couple is currently $34,000/year, but this cuts out if income-producing assets, including super, are over $853,000. A 'comfortable' retirement is considered to cost $60,977/year, according to the Association of Superannuation Funds of Australia (ASFA), which means holding $640,000 in assets (including super) and running down capital, or over $1.5m in super, without reducing capital and not claiming the pension. Your individual target will depend on many factors and can be discussed with a financial planner.

2   ABS.Gov.au
3   www.dss.gov.au/our-responsibilities/seniors/publications-articles/
    pension-review-background-paper

Unfortunately, average superannuation balances for retirees are only $271,000 for men and $157,000 for women, and mean averages are skewed by a small, but very wealthy, few. The median average is only $110,000 for men and $36,000 for women, or $155,000 for couples (the midpoint is higher for couples). This is in part due to superannuation not being around for their full working life.

Even if we take a 30-year-old earning $100,000/year and model their super balance to age 65, they will only get to $500,000. Salary sacrificing to the limit will take them to $1m, but all the additional contributions are locked in until at least age 60, which prevents any of it being used for early retirement.[4]

On the other hand, a couple can earn up to $74,000 between them outside of super and only pay $8,000 in tax = $65,000/year net. To earn that through property would require the following combined rent:

Weekly rent	$1,780
Mortgage	$0
Agent fees, bills and utilities/week	$355
Net weekly income before tax	$1,425
Annual income before tax	$74,000
Annual net income	$65,376

---

4   www.moneysmart.gov.au/superannuation-and-retirement/
    is-your-super-on-target

An income of $1,780/week equates to three properties each rented at $595/week, or six properties at around $300/week. To net more than $66,000/year, each $10,000 increase in net income would require another approximately $360/week in rent.

Our modelling suggests that it's possible for 30-year-olds on a career path to buy a home and build a good, cash positive property portfolio in 11–15 years. It's still possible for those on middle incomes, with lower cost-of-living expectations. These figures are very generic and not meant to constitute advice, but buying cash positive properties makes self-funded retirement a more realistic possibility.

How long will you live and what will you do?

For our own exit plan, one of the key questions we ask ourselves is, 'How long are we going to live?' There's a great website for this, https://mylongevity.com.au, which will give an estimate based on lifestyle and other factors as to how long a person might live. The figure is surprisingly long for most people who live a relatively healthy lifestyle. Although life expectancy is over 80, it grows as we get older and avoid dying off earlier on. It's becoming more common for people to live into their 90s. Once we understand how long we might live, we need to look at some of the additional costs we're going to have along the way.

The easy costs to think about are the costs of supporting ourselves – bills and regular living costs, plus travel, for those interested, or pastimes like golf, or having lunch and coffee with friends and family, or spoiling the grandkids. People often miss the cost of aged care and increased health care, especially if we've developed a taste for private health insurance, which can be prohibitively expensive as we age. We all know the impacts of ageing on the human body; things can break down and go wrong, with a higher likelihood of treatments. Medicare might not provide for knee replacements or hip replacements, which are often seen as voluntary or have an incredibly long waiting list. For any of those things that we want to get done more quickly, we're going to need money.

Then we need to look at how long can we can afford to live for. The government pension is only around $34,000 per year for a couple. This doesn't cover any accommodation and barely covers a basic cost of living. Of course, that's what it's designed to do. It's to make sure that people are not living in poverty, not that they're living comfortably. Depending on how much of our assets are held in super, it is still possible to get a pension, even for those that receive income from superannuation. That's likely to change in the future as there's more retirees and more and more people trying to claim a pension and get an income from their superannuation at the same time.

Superannuation is a fantastic vehicle in Australia. When superannuation is building up in the 'accumulation phase', the income in that fund is taxed at 15%. Once we put some, or all, of that money into the 'pension phase', that income is currently not taxed. Again, the government may try and change that in the future, but for now, if we've got a decent number of assets in our superannuation fund, then we can get a good amount of untaxed income later. Currently, $1.6 million is the most that each individual can have in a superannuation fund and get that benefit. Most of us won't get close to that figure, which is why we'll need our property portfolios and the rental income that we collect if we keep them.

What to leave behind

Our legacy plan – what we want to leave behind – is an important thing to consider. On the one hand, we might think we just need to support ourselves in retirement, but we might also want to think about whether to leave a house or an income or a trust fund for any children and grandchildren that we have. It's worth noting that school fees can be paid from most family trusts if that income isn't needed to cover our costs of living.

If we don't think about leaving a legacy upfront, then we might waste assets and sell them to pay down our own debts, when in fact we want to leave them to the family after we go. I mentioned trusts, because a family trust will outlive us. They typically last for at least 80 years. If a trust holds the assets, then it will still hold those assets after we depart. We get the benefit while we're alive, but then the family, or whomever we leave our estate to, gets the benefit when we go, without taking those assets into their own names. We have to make sure that the trusts are properly administered, either by a trusted family member or by a solicitor, but having assets held in trust is a great way of continuing on with building the wealth in the family after we're gone.

Anything in our own names will need to be willed to someone, as will control of the family trusts. We need to make sure that we know what we want to leave behind and what we're prepared to use up during our lifetimes.

The other part of our legacy may be separate from the money and the assets that we leave behind; I also want to talk a little bit about giving back. It's one thing to leave money to family and friends, but it's something else to have contributed to a clean water source or the education of somebody in another country. One of the things that we're big on is giving a proportion of our income to good causes. There are thousands and thousands of different causes out there, but we focus on a couple of them, mentioned in the final chapter.

Sell or keep your home in retirement

A recent study found that 76% of retirees would like to stay in their family home, with 71% claiming it would be a safety net if things went wrong. That still means a quarter or more of us might want to downsize or take a sea change by moving to the coast, or a tree change by moving to the country.

During our working lives, we need to live near jobs, which are often in big cities, but once we stop work that's no longer a requirement. Historically, we've seen property prices rise much more rapidly in cities, so a tree or sea change can mean buying a cheaper property and having a surplus.

Kelly and I have moved way more than most, so I know that some moves end up being positive experiences and some negative. My advice to anyone considering a major change and moving away from family, friends and routine is to try before you buy. In other words, for those considering a change, try renting in the desired area for 12 months before committing to making the move permanent. As we've covered in Chapter Four, buying and selling is very expensive.

Imagine a couple, Bob and Tina, selling their $1.5m home in the city and moving to the country, where they buy for only $700,000. They both love the fresh air and walking the dog, and Bob enjoys the quiet time. But Tina finds that friends are hard to come by, there's nothing much to do and she doesn't want to bother Bob all the time. They persevere for a couple of years, but Tina finally convinces Bob that she'd be happier back in the city. In the meantime, their country home value has flat-lined and city prices are up 10% to $1.65m. Let's look at the outcome for them:

	City to country	Country to city
Sale Price	1,500,000	700,0000
Sell Costs	35,000	15,000
Net	1,465,000	685,000
Buy Price	700,000	1,650,000
Buy Costs	35,000	80,000
Total	735,000	1,730,000
Surplus/Shortfall	730,000	1,045,000

Moving to the country gave Bob and Tina a $730,000 surplus, yet moving back required $1.045m, or $315,000 more than their previous surplus. Instead, they could have rented their home for more than the rent they would pay in the country. After one to two years, they could have come back, or made the move permanent, knowing it was the right thing to do.

The same goes for downsizing within the city. More and more empty nesters are looking to sell their family home and move into an apartment. For some, it's the best thing they've ever done, but others miss their gardens, their privacy and their extra space for when their kids and grandkids come to visit. If we plan to be retired for 20–30 years, taking one to two years to make a more informed decision about any major move is well worth it. We've helped several empty nesters borrow to buy a new property and keep their original. It's not as tax efficient with the debt being non-deductible, but it's allowed them to try out a new area. If they like it and stay, the old home can be sold and the debt cleared, or super can be used to clear the debt and they can live on the rental income. If it doesn't work out, they can move back to the old home and rent out the recently purchased one. Rent, savings or super can be used to pay off the debt.

As another example, Laura bought a home down the coast and kept her family home, renting it out for $1,000/week, or $52,000/year. Unfortunately, after deducting costs of around $12,000, she was left with $40,000 of taxable income. She was still enjoying working as a nurse and paid 39% in tax, leaving her with a $15,600 tax bill. Her income of $40,000 less $15,600 tax gave her only $24,400 in net rental. Her mortgage on the new place was costing her $36,000, so Laura felt like she was much worse off than she had been. We had to explain that while she was still working, she could pay down the debt on the new place, eliminating the mortgage in 20 years based on the scheduled repayments, or only 10 years by putting in what she could afford. Once Laura retires in 10 years' time, tax on the $40,000 income will drop to around $5,000, giving her $35,000 plus her super income to live on. She still has the option to sell later and draw a bigger income to support a more comfortable lifestyle.

As is often the case, the conclusion to the buy-or-sell question depends on individual circumstances, but my preference is always to keep first and reconsider later. Downsizing is tempting, and can help to clear other mortgages, but it's an irreversible decision. Keeping a property increases flexibility and may also give you the opportunity to leave it to the kids. Or the dogs' home, if you prefer.

Stage Five: Pay Down summary

Pay off owner-occupied debt first. The rates might look lower than those of other debts, but when we calculate the tax differences, we're normally better off getting rid of it. Then we can knock over the other debts using 50% of our income, instead of only 20%.

Build up as much money as possible in redraw or off-set, and $1m in cash would be lovely to have on hand, just in case.

Don't get caught out relying on the pension, like most people do.

Build a portfolio, one with a structure that will support you for all your remaining years and allow you to leave a legacy. If you want to sell the family home, do it as a last resort, after trying out the other alternatives first.

SIXTEEN

What Next

Congratulations on reaching this far in a book about money!

From here, the next steps are about taking action. Sadly, the law of inertia suggests that most people do nothing, so we will look at that first.

Then, we'll look at giving back, which can be a bigger motivator as we become so sure we can take care of ourselves that we can branch out into helping others. For every copy of this book sold, I make a donation to help others.

Doing nothing

This is our default mode. It's far easier to come up with excuses about why changing behaviours or getting out and doing something won't work than actually trying to see if it will. Ironically, one of the excuses I've heard for doing nothing is that if it were as straightforward as I've made it in this book, everyone would be doing it and it wouldn't work anymore. Well that's one less person we have to worry about competing with! Then again, it's easy to win against a couch potato, keyboard warrior or naysayer.

There's no hype or exaggeration in this book. You won't find me on the Financial Review Rich List, or pictured with a private jet. We really were from poor families. We still have relatives living in housing commission. We mismanaged our finances for eleven years and had to cope with the financial pressures of having three kids in our twenties. But we bought property, built a business and Kelly retired at 47. I'm constantly amazed at how far we've come and how lucky we are, and I take the time to appreciate the world around us. But I love to teach and hope that this book will inspire others to make the most of their lives, too.

In reality, we can't compete against anyone else, only against our own potential. Under-achieving against our own potential will be hugely disappointing in later life. If only we'd done this, or that, we'd be there and not here. To have got this far, you've already shown perseverance, curiosity and a willingness to learn. A journey of a thousand miles begins with a single step, so just take one. Take one single step forward by implementing the five-2 money diet. From then on, anything is possible.

Doing it yourself

Like many, I've often fallen into the trap of trying to do things myself. Surely I can figure it out. Surely I can save money if I do it myself.

No doubt it is possible to do everything by yourself, but if that's your aim then do it properly. Take the time to educate yourself with books, videos and seminars to learn as much as possible. We even offer free seminars precisely because we want to push DIY-ers further along their path.

But books, videos and seminars are no substitute for doing stuff – researching properties, trying new bank account structures, buying anything to get started. In the beginning, we don't know what we don't know. Then we realise the more we know, the more we know there is to know. Eventually we move onto knowing that we know something. But you know that you've made it when you realise that you're comfortably doing something that you didn't even notice other people had to do as part of their paths to success. That's when you need to take the time to remember what it was like in the beginning and try and write your thoughts down in a book.

One of the biggest motivations for me to write this book was meeting a much younger version of myself. I took on a young student, Christian, who was looking to work part-time while he finished his Economics degree. If only I'd known at his age what I know now. I've been inspired to share as much as possible with him over the past year, and every week he asks me a question about something I'd forgotten I knew and just took for granted. My wish for him and for my readers is that you can all learn from my mistakes and get to my level and beyond more quickly than I did. At 22, Christian is buying his first investment property, through his own family trust that he just created. By buying interstate through a trust, he won't be disqualified from the first home buyer benefits back in NSW. A year ago, he had no idea such a thing was even possible.

Getting help

It's a bit like asking for directions – when you know where you want to go, but feel a bit lost, ask for help. Makes perfect sense. The types of people that can help you out are:

Money coach – Not many of us around, but there are a few to choose from. Make sure your money coach is someone you can get along with and who understands your short- and long-term needs. Also check their situation and motivations. Anyone motivated solely by making money, or who hasn't started their own investment journey, should be avoided. A good money coach will help you to implement a personalised money management plan and give you practical tips on what your future steps will look like. Avoid property spruikers whose solution is selling you a property they are making a commission on, with a plan that could have been calculated by a year five student, such as 'Buy ten properties, wait for them to double and sell five.'

Financial planner – can be good for organising insurances and superannuation. Again, watch for their motivations and make sure a free consultation doesn't result in a $2,000–$3,000 fee for a 'financial plan' that you're not convinced you need. Make sure you know the likely content before agreeing to such a fee. If it's pure insurance, which pays commission, then the plan should be free, or the commission rebated.

Mortgage broker – can help with borrowing capacity and loan structuring and be a calming voice during the stresses of buying. A good rapport and track record is important. Also make sure their lender choices are many and varied and not restricted to just two or three lenders. Every new term and document should be well explained along the way, to help build your knowledge and reduce anxiety.

Solicitor – can help with conveyancing any property transactions and advise on the legal consequences of different structures. A solicitor can also help with family loan documents and, if necessary, binding financial agreements. Locality can be important, for document signing and face to face discussions. Lots of help and follow up are important. Ask about the number of contracts they will review during the purchase process and the cost for each. To buy one property may require document checking and negotiating on three or four others. If each auction has four bidders, three must have missed out after reviewing contracts, strata reports and negotiating contract changes.

Buyer's agent – an essential team member for any out-of-area purchase, and also worth considering to help with negotiations for a local purchase. Rapport and making sure they understand your needs are, again, important. This is still a relatively new field in Australia, so prices vary wildly. Access to different regions is important for portfolio building, as is understanding their bias and focus. Ask about their favourite purchases they've worked on and you'll get a sense of whether what they love and what you're thinking of are likely to be aligned.

Accountant – can advise on ownership structures and help set up trusts. Make sure they understand your long-term needs versus just trying to save you tax next year. Also ask who they recommend for depreciation schedules. Bizarrely, some will argue that they're not necessary, as claiming depreciation will impact capital gains. At the moment, such a statement would be at best 50% right; but if you hear such a thing, run.

Quantity surveyor – normally recommended by your mortgage broker or accountant. A good one will look up a property address and quickly tell you if it's worth their fee to draw up a full schedule for you. Ask how much it would cost if they found out there was nothing to claim.

General insurance broker – will make sure any landlord's insurance policies fit with your needs and lender requirements. A good mortgage broker will be able to refer you to one.

Property manager – critical for success with investment properties. These will typically be locally based. Each of my property managers looks after only one to three properties of mine, as the others would be out of their area. The best ones have standard contract terms with fees only charged while properties are occupied, or the fees are known items. They also have six-monthly inspections and rent reviews and send regular reports. The bad ones tend to be very cheap, seldom inspect your property and always ask what to do about problems without making a suggestion for the solution. All mine have a dollar limit that they have full discretion over, to spend on urgent or necessary repairs. I don't want an email asking if a leaking toilet should be fixed, only to find it went to junk mail and I missed it for the past few days. Of course it should be fixed, just include the bill in my next statement.

With a good team, hopefully coordinated by a good money coach or mortgage broker, it's amazing what can be achieved and how many pitfalls can be avoided. The biggest benefit of using a good team is typically time – both in terms of how quickly you can get started and also how much of your time gets eaten up during the property buying process.

Paying it forward

When we're young, it's tempting to do everything for ourselves and let everyone else worry about themselves. A former teaching colleague of mine, Henry Chitsenga, grew up in Zimbabwe before moving to the UK to teach maths. He always knew how lucky he was compared to the people back home, and every year he would go back and try to bring school supplies for kids and do sponsored events to help raise money for orphans and disabled children in Zimbabwe. At first, I used to give him some money for his sponsored events, but then I started trying to help him hit his goals by making up the shortfall or kicking off with a decent amount. I always reasoned that I could make more money and not really miss $1,000 as a one-off. He was always overwhelmed and thankful for those kinds of donations. Long after I'd moved back to Australia, Henry emailed me to let me know that the charity he worked with, Suchhope, could no longer afford to sponsor some of the students they had been supporting through university. He asked if I could make regular donations to cover fees and living expenses, since the universities were far from where the students came from. I agreed to sponsor one student, Brenda, three years ago, out of my travel budget, but Henry was desperate on behalf of another student, who had become depressed about the prospect of dropping out of uni. Fadzi had never known her father, and her mother died in childbirth when Fadzi was just fifteen. Her step-father disowned her, making it very difficult for her to continue studying. I put Fadzi's story to the other brokers from our company, Golden Eggs, and we agreed to sponsor her as a company. I also bought laptops for Brenda and Fadzi, to help them study. We had the laptops engraved, and Henry presented them at special ceremonies because it was such a big deal.

Fadzi graduated in 2018, but unemployment in Zimbabwe is very high, especially amongst women and those with no experience. We decided to hire her to help us in our loan business, working remotely from an office in Harare. Training her was difficult, due to the time difference and poor internet connection over there, so we decided to bring her to Australia for 12 weeks. It was her first flight and first time out of Zimbabwe, and after her first week of being here she still couldn't come to terms with people walking the streets after dark and feeling safe. Fadzi cannot believe how lucky she is, nor how an atheist would bestow her with such blessings she can only believe could come from God.

The impact we can have on the lives of others is incredible and reminds us of how lucky we are to have been born in such a prosperous country. We have taken the 1% pledge, so that 1% of all Golden Eggs' revenue goes towards the United Nations Global Goals for Sustainable Development. We use the B1G1 platform to make sure that everything we do can be linked back to a benefit towards education or poverty eradication in developing countries.

How you choose to give back is up to you, but just for getting a copy of this book we have donated on your behalf. If you know a 25- to 35-year-old on a career path who might be interested in knowing more, please put them in touch to get a copy of this book or to come to one of our workshops. For every person attending one of our free workshops that mentions this book, we will donate a month's education for a child in Zimbabwe.

I do hope this book has inspired you to take action, change some habits, or come and see us to find out more.

Either way, I really do mean it when I say: I hope that you live long, and prosper.

Acknowledgements

Robert Kiyosaki's book *Rich Dad, Poor Dad* inspired me to start reading again at age 32, for the first time since leaving school. Many of his other books have influenced my thinking since then.

I am grateful to Jenny and the team from Oxford University's Smith School of Enterprise and Environment for allowing me to use some of the graphs from their 2016 cross-country insurance study, conducted with Zurich.

On the subject of test readers, thanks especially to Sara Lassemilante for her page by page feedback, to Daniel Harrop for his interest and to Ian Dawson for his consistent support of everything at Golden Eggs.

Special thanks go to the team at Dent Global for their outstanding KPI programme that gave me the tools to write this and the accountability to follow through. Thanks also for reminding us of the importance of giving back.

To Henry Chitsenga of Suchhope.org, you are an inspiration to everyone who learns your story and I'm so grateful to you for staying in touch. You persuaded me to go from sponsoring your activities to sponsoring students directly, which led us to Brenda and Ropafadzu. I hope we can help many more students in the future.

Thanks for all the help from Lucy McCarraher and the whole Rethink Press team, without whom I'd be stuck with a badly over-worded book with a terrible cover.

I need to thank my dad, Charlie Phelps, for inspiring me to travel, teaching me to work hard but do the work you enjoy, and for somehow punching way above his weight to marry my mum, Josephine, sadly no longer with us. I know she would have loved to see herself mentioned in a book, written by one of her nine kids, and been proud to show copies to all her friends and tell anyone that would listen. I will forever be grateful to her for so many life lessons and always taking the time to listen. Nine children, twenty-seven grandchildren and one great grandson (my grandson) is a huge legacy to leave behind.

I wrote this book to share what I know, but also to make Matthew proud of his grandad. We've spent almost every Friday together since he was two months old and I will miss him when he starts school next year. I love his dad, Jack, and his uncles Josh and Daniel too, but Matthew has given me a fresh look at the world at a time in my life when I've been ready to look beyond the mundane.

Finally, to my wife Kelly, who has been by my side for almost 30 years now, I will be forever grateful that you've put up with me for so long. If you hadn't been so bad with money and learned to manage within our five-2 system, a lot of this book would not have existed. You help to balance off my idiosyncrasies so well that on average we appear normal. I look forward to spending the rest of my life dating you every week and travelling the world many more times over. If the book takes off, I might even fly up in business class with you occasionally!

The Author

Max grew up in a family of nine kids, playing Monopoly and aiming not to be poor. Initially terrible at saving, during a sales and marketing career with a multinational he stumbled across an effective set-up. He spent a couple of years as a maths teacher and began investing in property in order to retire young.

Now Max is a professional property investor, with ten years of experience in finance, and qualifications in mortgage broking and financial planning. These days he spends his time coaching 25- to 35-year-olds on how to get their money shit together – to become financially secure in order to make choices about their future happiness and retirement plans. He wants them to learn from the mistakes he made, yet gain the same – or greater – success. When he takes a break, it's to travel with the love of his life and partner for twenty-nine years, Kelly. On Fridays he is with his grandson, Matthew, and he cannot be disturbed.

Max has taken the 1% Pledge and every book purchased contributes to improving education and ending poverty in developing countries.

You can find him at:

in www.linkedin.com/in/goldeneggsmaxphelps

f www.facebook.com/moneyshit.info

⊕ www.goldeneggs.info